To dear Elaine and Chris,

In apprecia[tion]

wonderful hospitality and kindness t[o]

Warmest regards,

Vicki + John

GARDENS
IN TIME

GARDENS IN TIME

In the Footsteps of Edna Walling

TRISHA DIXON
JENNIE CHURCHILL

ANGUS
& ROBERTSON
PUBLISHERS

ANGUS & ROBERTSON PUBLISHERS

Unit 4, Eden Park, 31 Waterloo Road,
North Ryde, NSW, Australia 2113;
94 Newton Road, Auckland 1,
New Zealand; and
16 Golden Square, London W1R 4BN,
United Kingdom

First published in Australia
by Angus & Robertson Publishers in 1988
First published in New Zealand
by Angus & Robertson NZ Ltd in 1988

National Library of Australia
Cataloguing-in-publication data.

Churchill, Jennie, 1951-   .
  Gardens in time: in the footsteps of Edna Walling.

  Bibliography.
  ISBN 0 207 15750 2.

  1. Walling, Edna, 1896–1973. 2. Landscape gardening —
  Australia — History. 3. Gardens — Australia — History.
  I. Dixon, Trisha, 1953-   . II. Title.
712'.6'0924

Typeset in 10/14 Palatino by Best Set Typesetters
Printed in Singapore

Contents

Preface

EDNA WALLING is far from being just a memory, a collection of manuscripts and a bundle of faded photographs. Tangible evidence remains of the skills of the the woman who became one of Australia's most influential landscape designers. So evocative and inspirational are her writings, an aura of mystery and expectancy has come to surround her gardens.

This book set out to explore that mystery and to discover what, if anything, was left of her creations. Retracing her steps unearthed alternately treasures and disappointments. To wander through gardens that had been conceived sixty years ago and which had attained in their maturity such grace and harmony gave immense pleasure. Then again, so many were fading rapidly into neglect that it became a matter of great importance to us to record the few gardens that remained intact, of the hundreds she had designed.

This book is also about inspiration. For those who already know and love Edna Walling, it offers a chance to see her creations in their maturity, and for those who have yet to be touched by her spell, a tantalising glimpse into a world of romantic gardens.

Although a book of gardens, the people involved with those gardens have contributed enormously and enthusiastically: towards the research, with their hospitality, and by opening their gardens to us so readily.

Edna Walling's niece, Barbara Barnes, has given us unfailing encouragement and support, all the way from her property in Queensland, as well as granting us full use of all published and unpublished manuscripts. We are especially grateful to Peter Watts for his generosity in allowing us access to all his precious research notes on Edna Walling and her gardens. His material provided us with a starting point for our research. Margaret Carnegie has written a delightfully amusing and personal foreword, and Judy Baillieu, Brian McKeever and Glen Wilson deserve our special thanks for their wonderful assistance.

GARDENS IN TIME

During our research, we had the pleasure of visiting countless gardens and we are grateful to their generous owners. In particular, we would like to thank the patient owners who enabled us to photograph their gardens through the seasons: Mr and Mrs Frank Walker, Rae Rogers, Trish and Maurie Bull, Mr and Mrs Andrew Manifold, Mr and Mrs Jim Beattie, Mr and Mrs Laurie Ledger, Mrs Chester Guest, Mr and Mrs I. D. Mackinnon, Dame Elizabeth Murdoch, Mr and Mrs Geoff Ashton, Lady Carnegie, Mrs Sarah Myer, Mrs Elizabeth Rowe, Rowena McDonald, Miss Janet McClure, Mrs Robina Youngman, Mrs Freda Frieberg, Mrs Blanche Marshall, Mr and Mrs Dudley Cain, Mr and Mrs Houlihan, Joanne McWilliams, Mr and Mrs George Walsh, Mr and Mrs L. Wilson, Mr and Mrs W. Pont, and Pat Garrett from Government House. Helpful information was gratefully received from Mrs Weatherly, Mr M. A. Cuming, Helen Marshall, and many other individuals and groups too numerous to mention.

Acknowledgement is also given to those who have supplied plans for reproduction, including Peter Watts and Mark Strizic, the La Trobe Collection of the State Library of Victoria, Ron Berg and *Belle*, Garry Broome, Neil Robertson, Mrs Morson and many of the formerly mentioned garden owners. *Home Beautiful* has also kindly allowed reproduction of a plan and excerpts from Miss Walling's writings. We would also like to thank Margaret Hendry and Glen Wilson who lent the photographs of Edna Walling thought to have been taken by Miss Daphne Pearson. Thanks also to Henry Jolles who photographed many of the plans previously unpublished.

For help in research we acknowledge with thanks the Knox Historical Society, Ferntree Gully; the Lorne Historical Society and the Brighton Historical Society.

Further acknowledgement is extended to Mrs Simon Wincer, Mr and Mrs K. McDermott, Mrs Wills-Cooke, Mr J. Cooper, Mr and Mrs West, Mrs Margaret Barker, Mr and Mrs D. Nelson, Mr R. Gordon, Mrs Fletcher, Mr and Mrs Rayson, Mrs S. Mayes, Dr and Mrs Kirkwood, Mr L. Gough, Mr and Mrs P. Peppard, Mr and Mrs Hastie, Mr and Mrs H. E. Michell, Mr and Mrs Faragher, Mrs S. Ruhsam, Mr M. Armstrong, Mrs Noni Larritt, Mrs Stewart, Mr Eric Hammond, Tina Bain and B.H.P. Collieries Division.

Finally, our hitherto non-gardening husbands, Darvall and Rob have endured and shared our preoccupation with gardens, tripods and cameras, gardens, film in the fridge, gardens, apertures and exposures...and even more gardens.

TRISHA DIXON AND JENNIE CHURCHILL, 1988

Foreword

"You should have called me in to place the house," was Edna Walling's greeting when she arrived at Holbrook in 1948 to find the Kildrummie homestead half built. "Remember," she said, "I told you that before at Grant Avenue." She continued the lecture, "It is important to place a house correctly on its site."

It was a lesson my husband and I remembered years later when we built up another property, Water Park. This time, we called in our landscape architect, Victoria Grounds, while the house was still being planned.

Our first garden at 4 Grant Avenue was designed by Edna for us in 1937, in what I call her Gertrude Jekyll and Sir Edward Lutyens period. This was a period which then fitted my nostalgia for Europe and the grand English gardens of the eighteenth century. After the Second World War, however, my thoughts had changed. My husband and I had become, and remain, ardent Australian nationalists. Fortunately, Edna's views had also changed.

Patient hours were spent by Edna and my husband driving through the paddocks to define the sweep of the drive. "Always sweep up to a house in a curve, never in a straight line," was one of Edna's precepts.

As many patient hours were spent marking out the ha-ha and the curves of the rock walls which Rocky (the late Ellis Stones) would build to delineate the edges of the sweeping lawn. Rocky spent three months at the local hotel teaching our men to assist him building the ha-ha and the rock walls, which became a prominent feature of the garden.

Before that occurred, however, a hitch with a capital H developed. Douglas, a Rat of Tobruk just out of the army, had planned it all like a military operation. Mr Hammond and his men had arrived from Melbourne, the bulldozers were waiting to sculpt the earth under Edna's direction, while our men, with loads of huge boulders and rocks which they had brought down from the hills on a makeshift sleigh, were standing at the ready, when a telegram arrived from Edna: "Sorry, arriving a day later."

Furious, Douglas said, "We can't keep everyone standing by; we have to make a start."

When Edna arrived the following morning, she was equally furious that we had started. "The ballet," she said, "cannot begin without the principal ballerina, likewise the curtain cannot go up at the opera without the diva."

I became the meat in the sandwich between two sparring bulls. Somehow, I prevailed upon Edna to remain. Douglas then discovered she was delightful to work with after a mid-morning sherry, and I could relax while we happily discussed erosion and conservation problems.

The garden was to be essentially Australian, planted with native shrubs, and the driveway was to have the lovely soft blue-green *Eucalyptus cinerea*. Mr Schubert arrived with a truckload of native trees and shrubs to plant under Edna's watchful eye. Then she decided upon a deciduous pear tree to shade the western courtyard, and an old-fashioned apple tree to protect the office doorway from the morning sun. "Never prune them," she advised. Next, she placed the evergreen *Trachelospermum jasminoides* (Chinese star jasmine) to grow in the poor soil alongside the pisé walls beside the house and creep over the iron balustrade at the front door. We realised just how right her choice was in the summer, when the fruit trees provided welcome shade and the scent of the jasmine wafted through the house throughout the long summer months.

"Never water. If you do, you will have to continue," she warned. This warning we were to disregard two or three years later, as losses from the native shrubs mounted. Probably we should have persevered and thereby saved ourselves many watering hours.

Each of the gardens at Grant Avenue and at Kildrummie gave us enormous pleasure in the different periods of our lives, and their present owners still preserve and cherish them.

If our immortality rests in the hearts and minds of the people our actions influence, then Edna Walling's gardens, her philosophies and the principles she enunciated will ensure her place forever in the gardening history of Australia.

MARGARET CARNEGIE

A Brilliant Career

1896 – 1973

*E*dna Walling's influence on Australian gardens has been prodigious. This talented landscape designer, photographer, writer and conservationist has played a dominant role in the creation of gardens in this country since the 1920s. Through her prolific writings and sensitive sepia photographs, she is still inspiring gardeners long after her death.

Born in 1896 in Yorkshire, she brought to Australia strong memories of simple stone cottages, romantic flower gardens and long walks with her father through the soft English countryside. Her formative years instilled in the young Edna Walling basic principles that remained intrinsic to her future designs.

After a brief sojourn in New Zealand, the Walling family settled in Melbourne in 1912. Prompted by the unappealing prospect of an idle life, and encouraged by supportive parents, Edna went in search of her "life's work". With no definite aspirations, she enrolled at Burnley Horticultural College in 1916, perhaps inspired by romantic notions of the outdoor life... "all I longed for was the soil: what I was to do with it wasn't clear, nor did it bother me".

One of the first three women students to be admitted to full-time study at Burnley, her contemporaries and lecturers included Olive Mellor (née Molltum) and Milly Gibson (née Grassick). Like Edna, these women shared a British childhood and must have carried with them the strong traditions of English gardening.

Despite being recorded as a capable and hardworking student, Edna was ambivalent towards her studies and the resultant graduation certificate. Nevertheless, her independent and energetic nature led her to take a job as a garden labourer. Two years later, disheartened by her decreasing enthusiasm for gardens, inspiration came from the sight of "a stone wall supporting a semi-circular terrace;...I was fascinated...'I shall build walls,' I found myself solemnly registering." At last there was direction in her life, and this simple stone wall motivated her to develop the skills in garden construction and design that were to become a particular Walling characteristic.

A simple request to an architect acquaintance that she design a garden around his latest house led to a burgeoning career. Edna Walling rapidly became one of the most sought-after landscape designers in Victoria. In strong contrast to the largely formal designs she was executing during these early years, her personal life revolved around a small stone cottage surrounded by old-fashioned flowers and bushland at Mooroolbark. Sonning satisfied her desire for independence and her love of building, giving her the chance to demonstrate the rewards of constructing homes in harmony with their surroundings. By the early 1920s, this idea was extended to the creation of a village, and she purchased an adjacent eighteen acres (seven hectares) for subdivision. Blanche Sharpe (later Marshall), friend and bookkeeper, noted in her diary on 11 October 1928, ''...called the place Bickleigh Vale''.

By now, commissions were pouring in from all over Victoria and occasionally interstate. Her designs from this period, superbly illustrated in watercolour, were predominantly symmetrical and axial, containing strong architectural elements. Inspired by gardeners such as Gertrude Jekyll, Miss Walling favoured the great English tradition of a solid underlying framework softened by prolific and exuberant planting. Creating this framework gave her the greatest pleasure, more so than the planting: ''Once the walls, stairways and terraces were completed the planting had to be faced of course, and I was sufficiently interested in my new garden not to have it spoilt by planting that I did not like. Always I have longed for a collaborator to whom I could hand over this side of the garden making while I got on with more building.''

Despite these protestations, she had an enormous and detailed knowledge of plants, and delighted in describing new and old treasures. In *A Gardener's Log*, Miss Walling writes of walking in the

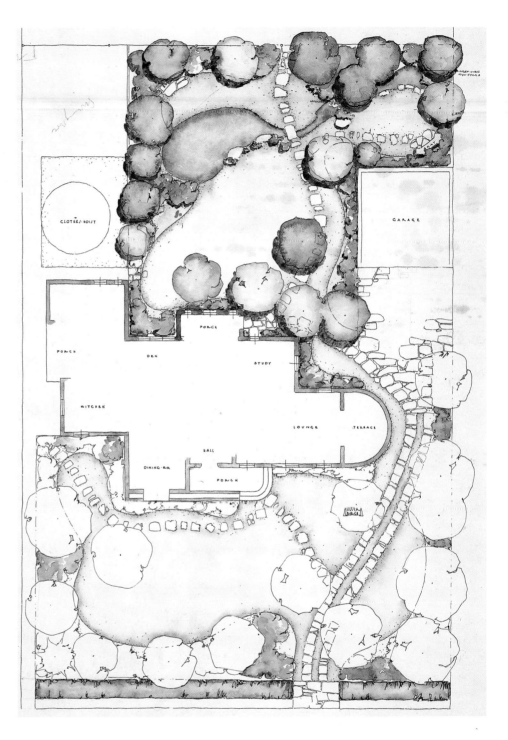

Grampians where she came ''face to face with thousands of Baeckias and the shell-pink Boronia. I just sat down and gazed and gazed. To have seen anything so exquisitely beautiful before one dies seemed to be all that mattered!'' For all her independence of spirit, she was an incurable romantic.

The lasting impression created by Miss Walling's mode of dressing was anything but romantic. Jodhpurs, gaiters and boots were standard dress for this practical and hardworking woman. Collar and tie, a short boyish haircut and a hat completed the picture. Another side emerged, however, as one client recalls: "She was tireless when working in the garden, digging in her jodhpurs and placing pegs for trees. But at the end of the day, a hot bath, and there was Edna Walling in black velvet with lace collar. One couldn't believe it was the same person, but what an enchanting one."

Always a lady, Edna nevertheless threw herself wholeheartedly into the manual side of garden construction, and in fact appeared to enjoy the opportunity for indulging in "hands on" stone work. She tended to be totally involved in the making of a garden, from the design through construction to the actual planting. Her enthusiasm for hard work made an impression on many of her clients, who frequently recalled her strength, stamina and unflagging energy.

Miss Walling was strong-willed and spirited, and not all her relations with her clients were amicable. It was no doubt difficult for many of her powerful and wealthy male clients to bow to this determined young woman who dared to wear men's apparel. She could also be testy with her friends, on occasion. Enlightening entries in Blanche Marshall's sparsely kept diary read on successive days in 1929, "Edna ghastly", "Edna unbearable" and "Sonning, doing the books, Edna deserted me". Despite these lapses, she inspired unswerving loyalty among friends and followers.

This loyalty was exemplified in the business relationship between Edna Walling and Eric Hammond, the landscape contractor who worked harmoniously with her for forty years with "never an argument". His first commis-

sion, in 1927, was to construct the gardens Edna Walling had designed for the bear lawn (no longer in existence) at the Melbourne Zoo. With a team of up to ten men to oversee, he had to travel widely, often working on three gardens simultaneously. His forté was his superb

stonework, which is today often the only evidence of a Walling garden left intact.

Ellis Stones was another who benefited from Edna Walling's patronage. Perceptively recognising his latent talent as a stoneworker, she encouraged this young builder to change careers. Specialising in creating natural rock outcrops while working with Edna Walling, he went on to forge his own highly successful career in landscape design.

Glen Wilson had the opportunity to study under her in the 1950s. He recalls her "genius", particularly in respect to her use and manipulation of space and her superb sense of balance, proportion and scale. She emphasised to him the importance of learning to "sculpt the surface" when designing gardens, a reference to the success with which she utilised changes in level. Glen Wilson admired her innate ability to produce swift designs. Taking few notes, she would grasp quickly the feeling of a location and the salient points of her design. These sparse notes were transformed into exquisite watercolour plans, which are treasured today as works of art. Her free and relaxed way of drawing developed rapidly, and by the mid 1920s her distinctive style of presentation had already matured. Late in her career, she settled for rapid pencil sketches on brown paper, few of which survive. The actual task of designing and drawing was always accompanied by music — she had a deep love of the classics and professed to gain much inspiration from Beethoven.

Misconceptions remain regarding Edna Walling's professional fees. Records show her personal charge for services rendered to be usually the smallest part of the total account, which in a large garden encompassed high costs of labour, construction and plant material. (The construction of the extensive stonework in the garden at Mawarra was reputed to have cost two thousand pounds.) It was fortunate she favoured a frugal and simple lifestyle, as her financial status belied years of hard work.

The period in her life from the 1920s through the 1940s was exceedingly busy and fruitful. As well as the numerous gardens she was designing, Miss Walling was involved in the ongoing development of Bickleigh Vale, her nursery at Sonning was thriving, she was contributing to the magazine *Australian Home Beautiful* and developing expertise in photography.

A skilled and often adventurous photographer, Edna's faithful Rolleiflex travelled everywhere with her. She used this precision-made German, twin-lens

reflex camera, without a light meter, to great effect. In later years, her refusal to move into colour amused her friends, but perhaps revealed her perception of the aesthetic appeal of black and white. A darkroom (often improvised) was essential to her developing and processing. Photography was not only a much-loved pursuit — as a means of educating her gardening public, it rivalled in importance her writings. Always evocative, her photographs captured the essence of her design philosophies.

Miss Walling was featured in the 1986 publication *Australian Women Photographers 1840–1960*, and her work shows her mastery of subjects other than the gar-

den. Her sensitive self-portrait provides a fitting cover for the book.

By the age of thirty, she was writing a regular column in *Australian Home Beautiful* which continued for eight years. Through this medium, she influenced a growing public. Gardeners whose skills lay in producing manicured beds of massed annuals learned the delights of subtle colours, old-fashioned perennials, and shrubs and trees planted in natural groupings. Readers unable to afford the services of a landscape designer were able to request a plan, one of which was published in each issue. Despite her hectic schedule, Edna still found time to execute these plans in watercolour.

So endearing were her writings that her first book, *Gardens in Australia*, published in 1943, was an immediate success. Within seven years, four editions had been printed. *Cottage and Garden in Australia* followed in 1947, and a collection of her *Home Beautiful* articles was published in *A Gardener's Log* in 1948. These early books are now collector's items. *The Australian Roadside*, published in 1952, propounds her growing concern with conservation issues and *On the Trail of Australian Wildflowers*, published posthumously in 1985, continues that theme.

Edna Walling's involvement in environmental disputes began early in her career. Frequent letters to newspapers and her prolific writings, published and unpublished, exhorted the general public and government bodies to take a stand for the Australian environment. These issues, together with her immense love and knowledge of the natural bushland, led in the 1950s to a dramatic change in her planting style. She now became almost fanatically devoted to native flora. This, coupled with a more

restrained economic climate, resulted in a less structured garden design.

In the midst of a busy professional career, the peace of Edna's life among friends at Bickleigh Vale must have provided welcome respite. The pleasures of living in this simple English-style village had never diminished. Unfortunately, the increasing intrusions from encroaching suburbia eventually became intolerable, and so she made the tearing decision to leave her village. In 1967, at the age of 71, she started a new home and garden in Buderim, Queensland, enjoying the climate and the visits of her niece, Barbara Barnes. From her home, Bendles, she wrote of the rediscovered delights of a cottage garden: "Oh yes, this garden of mine is not going to be a fashionable one of native plants, much as I love natives. My garden will be stuffed full of as many of the old-world flowers as I can find that will thrive happily in this rather humid climate."

Following her sad exit from Victoria, her indomitable spirit rebounded with earlier, postponed plans for an Italian-inspired village in the warmth of her new surroundings. These plans had to be curtailed as poor health began to plague her. After several strokes and enduring the frustrations of a nursing home, she died on 8 August 1973.

During her life, Edna Walling produced an impressive number of unique and individual designs, each suited to a particular site and purpose. Her design elements may seem disparate — she wrote of her love of Italian and Spanish gardens, of cottage and native gardens, while the influence of traditional English gardening on her work was obvious — but there were, nevertheless, common threads linking these apparently varied styles, the most notable being her handling of architecture and planting. Always there was a structural framework, very strong and geometric in her formal designs, with even her simplest cottage gardens containing stone paths and low retaining walls. Her excellent sense of proportion and attention to detail resulted in construction that remains inspirational. She believed that good architecture enabled her gardens to survive. Even in the saddest and most neglected Walling gardens today, that hint of a retaining wall, those old stone steps smothered in ivy and that line of terraces glimpsed beneath years of undergrowth, can evoke a feeling of magic.

Edna took her inspiration for planting from nature. Finding little beauty in gaudy colours and vulgar variegation of leaf, she loved all shades of green, excelled in blending foliage, shape and texture, and always grouped her trees and shrubs. Self-seeding was encouraged, pruning was not, and only the most rampant growth was curbed. She strove for a natural effect, and her deep love and study of the Australian bush taught her valuable lessons on achieving a happy and thriving mix of plant material.

The talent lay then in blending the two — architecture and planting — and in this she succeeded brilliantly. Regardless of the design style she was emphasising, she aimed always for gardens that were harmonious and serene.

The philosophies and genius of this remarkable, creative woman have influenced a vast number of Australians. She was undoubtedly the catalyst for much change in the fields of gardening and conservation, and she left behind a wealth of written and photographic material for future generations to ponder.

Her personal creed and driving force were equally impressive and are best described in Miss Walling's own words, written of her last home, Bendles, and Mt Buderim... "I only hope I shall not be merely taking up the air, but shall contribute in some small way to the preservation of its natural beauty."

Bickleigh Vale

MOOROOLBARK
1920 – 1945

□ Trees grown wild in the old nursery behind The Barn.

Opposite: A glimpse of Downderry through a thicket of elms, robinia and prunus.

ickleigh Vale village: a name surrounded by romance, history and controversy. Dreamy notions of English hamlets and cottage gardens inspire a feeling of anticipation on approaching the village. Entering the narrow and leafy lanes, the sense of escape from suburbia is immediate. How enticing are the glimpses of brown and white painted cottages through dense foliage, and how exciting to read the quaint and familiar names etched into hewn timber on the simple field gates — Downderry, The Barn, Devon Cottage, Badger's Wood and Sonning — names synonymous with the magic of Edna Walling. In the eyes of Edna Walling's public, Bickleigh Vale has become the essence of her desire to create harmony between home and landscape.

Change is inevitable. Purists decry the modern additions to the cottages and structural changes to the gardens. Residents of the village defend these disparities from the original, saying an eight square cottage is impractical for a growing family and maturing gardens must ultimately attain a different character. Regardless of the differences, there remains an undeniable feeling of peace and seclusion in the village.

Bickleigh Vale had its beginnings as early as 1920, when Edna Walling, a young graduate from Burnley Horticultural College, purchased farmland at Mooroolbark, on the outskirts of Melbourne. "Three acres [about one hectare] of grazing land were secured, on which stood a few rather depressing she-oaks, and I began at once to fence it about to keep off the marauding cattle."

On this land, she built her first home, Sonning, a simple and rustic cottage utilising local stone and materials. Built as economically as possible, it nevertheless met her standards of proportion and character.

How often the inexperience of youth is responsible for creations that have been worth the struggle and yet would never have been attempted in later years. In blissful ignorance I commenced to build myself a house! It did not even occur to me that I knew nothing about it — and what a good thing it did not; and how fortunate was I in my parents. My father was a most practical man, but he did not remark that I was embarking on something about which one needed a little experience, to say the least; neither did he remind

me that I had no money. No, he sat in his chair and listened patiently to my youthful prattlings when I came home full of my land, and quietly remarked: "There are some fine packing cases at the works that might be useful to you; I'll send them up." The cottage was as good as built, I felt, and on one glorious day of excitement the cases arrived at the railway station, three miles [five kilometres] away. When you are young and have no money the mind works quite differently than in older years, when you have a banker who will make money available.

In the early 1920s, eighteen acres (seven hectares) surrounding Sonning came up for sale. Fearful of intrusions on her newly found tranquillity, Edna borrowed heavily to purchase the land and embarked upon a remarkable excursion into subdivision that was far ahead of its time.

I could not afford to own it, but I could control its destiny, and so it was decided that if built upon it must be, I would do the building. And now the little cottages nestle into a landscape set about with lovely-foliaged trees and hedges of flowering shrubs between, with quiet people happily working in their gardens.

Her determination to create a unique village, despite limited funds, shows the calibre and foresight of this strong-willed and free-thinking young woman. Even today, such harmonious rural residential developments are uncommon, and only rarely does a single person become so totally involved in guiding such a concept to reality.

Edna's involvement extended to the unusual practice of approving prospective purchasers, who had to agree to a cottage and garden of Miss Walling's design. Trees and shrubs were supplied freely from her nursery at Sonning, and personal interest was taken in the development of each garden. By the 1930s, the original paddocks were acquiring the charm of an English village.

In 1936, Sonning burnt to the ground, along with original manuscripts, precious books, photographs and all Edna's personal belongings. It was a measure of her strength that she spent that night designing Sonning II.

> *It should be emphasised that these blocks are only for those interested in English cottage design, the planting of trees and shrubs and the preservation of the existing landscape.*
>
> *Home Beautiful* Nov 1930
> — titled "Adventure in Landscape Gardening"

Miss Walling's book *Cottage and Garden in Australia* describes in much detail the building of her new home. Her opening sentence, "This cottage has been made up as we went along," belied her by now definite ideas on proportion and detail. Still using natural building materials where possible, Sonning II nevertheless had a totally different character to the original Sonning. By now, she was able to afford a larger home and such relative extravagance as Californian redwood shingles on the roof. Much was made of the correct proportions of windows and doors, the heights of ceilings, and roof lines, all aimed at creating a cottage of restful simplicity.

□ The autumn foliage of *Amelanchier canadensis* (**opposite**); Bickleigh Vale Road, reminiscent of an English country lane; a mature silver birch shelters a Walling-made birdbath; a charming and oft-used potting shed.

It is desired that all the cottages will be screened and sheltered with trees and shrubs, so that each will appear to be the only one on the landscape to those living within, except perhaps for a tiny peep of some distant stone chimney or a thread of blue smoke curving up from another.

Home Beautiful Nov 1930
— titled "Adventure in Landscape Gardening"

☐ Simple cottages now nestle amongst sixty years of growth.

Occasionally, aesthetics overruled practicalities, as in the entrance hall, "in which is situated a seventeen and a half inch wide [forty-five centimetres] stairway, subject of much expostulation on the part of not-so-sylph-like visitors".

Such was Edna's desire to achieve a total effect, the interior furnishings were no less important: "It's just as well to make up one's mind at the beginning — is it to be an old curiosity shop, or is the cottage to be a restful place of retreat?"

There will be thickets of Birches and Poplars and groups of Lilacs and Spireas.

Home Beautiful Nov 1930
— titled "Adventure in Landscape Gardening"

Furniture was spartan in the extreme, scrubbed bare planks serving as tables, and stools made from thick pieces of wood with heavy tea-tree sticks for supports. "A meal set on bare boards can be very inviting; a tight bunch of flowers from the cottage garden and 'white plates and cups, clean gleaming, ringed with blue lines'." Even the cottage china was considered an integral part of the overall scheme.

She loved recycling and adapting used materials — the kitchen sink at Sonning II was an old kauri laundry trough. "An amazing assortment of old timber forms the walls and fills the gables" of the garage, thoughtfully "placed to suit the trees which were there first", and "painted over with the scrapings of old paint pots, the colour is so nondescript that it is quite inconspicuous".

By 1951, Sonning II had become too large for Miss Walling and she chose to move into The Barn (originally Good-a-Meavy). Earlier designed as a stable, garage, feed and harness room with workshop and man's room above, it was also used as her photographic darkroom. The Barn was constructed in 1929 for a meagre twelve pounds, with building materials that included motor packing cases, a few loads of stone, timber and galvanised iron. Despite the frugality of the original budget, it was an unusual and charming building, featuring a central open breezeway. Welcoming the opportunity to indulge in construction, Miss Walling, at this time aged 55, built the chimney during The Barn's conversion to a cottage. It was to be her last home in the village.

Bickleigh Vale now comprised sixteen cottages. It was a community of like-minded people who shared especially a love of gardening. Simple gates linked each garden, adding to the fellowship of the village. One long-time resident recalls Miss Walling still being a strong force in the village as late as the 1960s, striding between gardens proffering advice.

A new generation was now moving into the village, a generation of young, growing families with differing needs. Downderry, originally built for Edna Walling's mother, became home to a young architect, Brian McKeever. Having known Miss Walling during his childhood at Badger's Wood in the village, he was in sympathy with her original concept. He became the logical choice as architect for most of the additions carried out on the tiny cottages. When he consulted Miss Walling with beautifully drawn plans for the extensions to Downderry, she made the

☐ Details of The Barn, Edna Walling's last home in the village: *impatiens* and terracotta pots soften paving; perennial beds overrun with white cosmos, shasta daisies and the single, pale pink Japanese anemones; oak and robinias frame the front façade.

immediate comment, "You have no morning sun in your bedroom — Jan [his wife] won't like that!" Like most people with whom she came in contact Brian felt Miss Walling's influence.

Modern alterations have been a natural extension of the existing cottages. Roof lines, external cladding, and window and door proportions have been carefully maintained. Although much larger, the cottages retain their individual characters. Brian felt Miss Walling accepted these changes as a logical progression in the growth of the village.

"Winty has grown up," was her pleased comment when one of her cottages was enlarged.

The villagers today maintain they are still part of a close community, trying to preserve the ethos of the original concept. This is becoming increasingly difficult. Suburban encroachment, which in 1967 caused Miss Walling to leave in despair for Queensland, has continued relentlessly. The village has become a pocket in the midst of urban development, a remnant tied to the past.

In realistic terms, what are its chances

of survival? And with whom does the responsibility lie? The village is on the register of The National Estate, the inventory of the Australian Heritage Commission. The National Trust lists it as a "classified landscape", while the Upper Yarra Valley And Dandenong Ranges Authority designates the village as being of "high regional historical significance". The latter categorisation carries the strongest weight and is largely responsible for the current change of zoning by the Shire of Lilydale Council. The minimum subdivision area has doubled from half an acre (a quarter hectare), a tree preservation Act now covers the village, and quite stringent covenants are in force regarding any proposed future development or alteration to topography and buildings. Another threat comes from the State Electricity Commission, which has been reported as being substantially responsible for the deterioration of roadside vegetation in the village. Ultimately, however, it is the residents themselves who assume final responsibility for its future.

The wonderfully peaceful and rural atmosphere that pervades the village today, despite the inevitable intrusions of development, says a great deal for Edna Walling's foresight, determination and imagination. It is the fervent hope of those who know and love Bickleigh Vale village that all who touch it, do so with the utmost thought for its preservation. Bickleigh Vale has been recognised as having important regional significance, but it is more than that — it is the realisation of the far-sighted dream of one of Australia's foremost landscape designers, and as such is unique and irreplaceable.

A Box Hill Garden

A little plant which never fails to thrive in almost every situation is Erigeron mucronatus, *commonly known as babies' tears.*

□ Simple stone steps lead into this early city garden.

Opposite: A pleasing juxtaposition of foliage, colour and texture — spireas, babies' tears and ornamental grape.

"Steps and stairways! What delightful fancies with which to idly play. What could be more romantic than a formal garden stairway or more intriguing than brief steps of boulders? And with what precision and care these things must be designed," wrote Edna Walling in *Gardens in Australia*.

It was with such precision and care that the steps leading into this tiny suburban Melbourne garden were built in the early 1920s. Softened by babies' tears, a delicate but hardy *Erigeron* much favoured by Edna Walling for its propensity to self-seed, this stonework holds important architectural interest.

Most of the original trees survive, the most outstanding being an aged crab-apple with dark plum coloured blossom. This species was developed at the Burnley Horticultural College where the young Edna Walling studied. The garden's original owner, Mr Hannaford, was friendly with a member of staff at the college, who no doubt recommended Miss Walling for the work.

Writing in *A Gardener's Log*, Miss Walling felt that entrance gardens should give a sensation of rest.

There is nothing very restful about masses of annuals, conjuring up as they do, hours of labour, and much expenditure on seed, fertilisers and water...I always feel that the more brilliant garden displays should, whenever possible, be kept for the rear of the house. There are, of course, those who prefer to display their horticultural powers and wares for all who pass to see; and there are those who have not thought that there are other and more interesting ways of dealing with the area between street and house than with standard roses and annuals; and to the latter, I suggest trees and lawn and evergreen shrubs to conceal the boundaries.

Unlike many of her other early and more elaborate Toorak gardens, this Box Hill garden is effective in its simplicity. Stepping stones wander across the central lawn to the front verandah and ground covers are encouraged to spill over formal stonework. Rather than a riot of colour, the mixed boundary planting of trees, shrubs and ground covers creates a subtle blend of foliage textures and greenery.

The Grimwade Garden

T O O R A K
1 9 2 6

E dna Walling's penchant for formality is superbly manifest in the Toorak garden she designed for Mr and Mrs John Grimwade in 1926. There is a common misconception that all Walling creations have a feeling of wildness, rusticity and total informality, with sweeping curves, unmown grass and copses of silver birch. This garden, like many of her early town gardens, displayed her genius for using strong architectural features to create designs that endure. Writing in *A Gardener's Log* in 1948, she described her approach to smaller gardens:

I have come to the conclusion that very small gardens have to be *constructed*, that is, the need for constructional features such as low walls, wall fountains, steps and pools is more vitally important than in an expansive garden where long vistas, variety in foliage texture, wide sweeps of lawn and grassy glade are more easily achieved. A small area *must* be more elaborated — not elaborate individual features, but designed to produce a variety of pictures that costly town properties should provide. It is all very well to lay out a simple rustic little garden that is a delight while it is young and fresh, but the time comes when such a garden ''goes off'' and then one looks around for another scheme that will never let you down.

Creating garden pictures was considered by Miss Walling to be a most important part of garden design. Each area of this beautifully maintained garden is a separate entity, a garden within a garden.

A driveway lined with iceberg roses and *ioensis* crab-apples leads into an enclosed courtyard. An aged cedar, existing even in 1926, leans over the large expanse of grey paving, white walls and grey slate roofs. Snow-in-summer and white foxgloves soften the base of this towering tree.

Inside the garden, stone paving leads from an open rectangle of lawn, and pauses briefly in a small green pocket of garden. Broad, low steps intersect the lawn, which runs to the base of a wall fountain smothered in climbing fig. Two large clipped *Buxus* mark the entry to the sunken lawn overhung by flowering crab-apples and cherries, scented climbers and dense evergreens. An elegant high-backed stone seat and a small lily pond focus interest on this enclosed retreat. Pale pink wisteria drapes the gracious white columns of the house façade which rise from huge clumps of

□ The aged cedar towers over the formal entrance court.

Opposite: The subtle greens and whites of cherry, viburnum and azaleas overhang this classic pool in the lower sunken garden.

☐ The elegant stone bench facing the pool in the lower garden. White columns, draped in pale wisteria and ornamental grape, rise from swathes of French lavender.

☐ **Opposite:** Sunlight catches the *Erigeron* in the cracks of the wall foundation. Such architecture provided focal points in Miss Walling's formal town gardens. White primulas at the foot of the stone bench.

French lavender, while fragrant jasmine hangs like a mantle on a rear wall.

This abundant planting around such a formal design was Miss Walling's way of gently clothing architectural framework — "the planting of a formal garden can utterly ruin it. This is one of the most difficult tasks, for to be a success the planting should be mostly informal, so that it becomes the softening influence that is so necessary to the formal design."

All the herbs seem particularly appropriate to the country garden. Observing, "I simply must have huge bunches of lavender and rosemary on which to dry my handkerchiefs," someone once conjured up a picture of a perfect country garden.

She goes on to say that, "the planting of a formal garden should almost entirely conceal the formality in construction in the height of the growing season", and that, "in winter there should still be the softening growth of evergreens to break up some of the constructional lines of walls and pergolas".

The calibre of the landscape designer was clearly visible even at such an early stage in her career. This mature design was produced just eight years after Edna graduated from Burnley Horticultural College and today remains, almost totally intact, as one of her earliest surviving gardens.

Gulls Way

FRANKSTON
1927

☐ White foxgloves and lilies mark the pathway down to the wild garden.

Opposite: Forget-me-nots flower freely at the base of a silver birch, typifying the simplicity of planting in this holiday retreat.

*T*his quiet and unassuming garden in Frankston is particularly interesting when viewed alongside Miss Walling's other gardens from the 1920s. The plan is extremely simple and totally informal — in direct contrast to her professed love of formality for town gardens — and was obviously intended as a low-maintenance holiday-cottage garden. Designed in 1927, it was commissioned by a Mrs Hamer who resided in Toorak. The property, was in fact, without permanent residents until 1960, when it became home for three keen and appreciative gardeners.

Its survival may well be due to the fact that its earlier owners could afford a live-in caretaker-gardener while devoting their own gardening energies to their town residences.

The inclusion of so many native plants in such an early Walling design is also notable. It perhaps shows her appreciation even then of the relaxed and informal atmosphere indigenous plants can create, and of their eminent suitability for seaside gardens. Inevitably, much of the planting has changed. The garden outlines, however, with their dominance of green punctuated only by the subdued pastels of foxgloves, lilies and daisies, have been remarkably preserved.

The site slopes steeply, with the garden hugging the side of a hill. The casual curves of the garden fade into long grass and stepping stones, leading down to huge drifts of white lilies that crowd the stream at the bottom of the garden.

A charming example of Miss Walling's simpler designs, it demonstrates even now her philosophies on planting: "The plants were nice and thick, the ground was well covered, and there was an air of wildness about the garden. It was the sort of garden in which you could garden if you wanted to but if you didn't it would not matter." (*A Gardener's Log*)

The present residents of Gulls Way have come to love this garden, especially its feeling of perpetual calm when outside, the sea gales are in constant motion.

Little Milton

TOORAK
1927

L ittle Milton is built on what was once the driveway of the Myer property, Whernside. In the early 1920s, the Moran family of Toorak sent the young female architect Muriel Stott to England, where she was commissioned to take measured drawings of Great Milton, an estate in Oxfordshire.

Hidden behind a rustic timber fence in Toorak, Little Milton is a small-scale replica of this stately English home, minus the stables. To complete the atmosphere, the equally young landscape architect Edna Walling was commissioned to design the garden.

The property changed hands in 1976, and, in a happy coincidence, the new owners contacted Eric Hammond to work on the garden, without knowing he had done the original construction work. Sympathetic to the atmosphere of their new residence, when the derelict gardener's cottage had to be dismantled, they utilised every roof shingle and brick from it in a new extension to the house.

This garden and home were featured in an article by Edna Walling in *Australian Home Beautiful* of May 1929. In it, she commented on the interesting arrangement of bricks in the pathways. Their soft red colour blends well with the large two-storey home, now weathered to a rich terracotta and softened by Edna Walling's design. Her highly favoured practice of dense boundary planting provides privacy and seclusion, particularly from the busy road beyond its front gate,

and the tall canopy gives a sense of scale to this grand home.

I never cease to be thrilled when entering my own gateway and always feel that entrance gardens should give the first sensation of rest to those returning home.

In many of her gardens the structural details have long since disappeared, but here the pergola and pool still remain, as do a number of her earthenware bird baths and pots. Sixty years of growth has smothered the pergola with wisteria which scents the paths and tennis court with a delicate fragrance in spring.

□ Different paving patterns add interest to the soft red bricks which complement the preponderance of greens in this secluded Toorak garden.

24

☐ This grand home is a small scale replica of the stately English manor Great Milton in Oxfordshire. Edna Walling's simple design offsets this grandeur. A rustic paling gate invites exploration of a thicket of poplars at the edge of the tennis court.

In the Walling tradition, Little Milton has an air of abstraction and gentle untidiness much loved by its owners. Later planting has, of necessity, become largely shade-loving, but has been kept soft and simple. Dense evergreen ground covers edge the brick paths and hang over the small pool, small *Erigeron* tumbles over the steps leading to the tennis court, and the gargoyle on a wall fountain peeps out of a tangle of ivy. Behind the tennis court, a hidden part of the garden is more reminiscent of the forgotten corner of a large country estate. Here a grove of mature poplars carpets the ground in autumn with soft golden leaves.

The garden has been allowed to develop naturally over the years and to adapt to the shade of the tall and maturing trees. Understated planting complements the grand architecture of the house, resulting in a home and garden that have aged together gracefully.

☐ Silver birch leaves carpet a pathway in autumn. The remnant of a wall fountain, this weathered gargoyle peers from a tangle of ivy.

Durrol

MT MACEDON
1928

□ This sundial and its sun-dappled
terrace is the central pivot in this
Italianate design. Moss-covered steps and
terraces overhung by lush foliage lend a
feeling of antiquity and mystery.

*T*here is pure magic and romance in the sunken garden at Durrol. If ever there was a hideaway where plant spirits and fairies could find delight, this mossy world buried at the bottom of the garden would surely enchant them. The visual impact of every imaginable shade of green, the harmonious blend of so many foliage textures, and the restrained symmetry of design, inspire a strong feeling of tranquillity which deepens as the garden descends the hillside.

Curving stone steps softened by forget-me-nots lead to the first terrace, where a circular garden is still flooded with light despite the maturity of the surrounding planting. Moss-covered steps descend further to a central sundial which these days is touched only by filtered sunshine. Symmetrical beds set into soft grey paving are shaded by a canopy of mature trees. At their feet, lush hellebores and lilies revel in the moist and shady conditions, and tall evergreen shrubs conceal the garden beyond, completing the feeling of total seclusion.

A simple green gate draws the eye and invites exploration to the lowest terrace. Sunshine once again floods the paddock beyond, revealing distant vistas between the trunks of towering eucalypts native to Mt Macedon.

This cloistered world of Miss Walling's design seems already steeped in antiquity, yet it is less than a century old. The plan, commissioned in 1928 for Mr and Mrs Stanley Allen, incorporated a steeply sloping site on the perimeters of an already established garden.

Edna Walling's involvement in the construction of this terraced garden resulted in slight changes to the original design. Her flexibility during the process of garden making was well known and was governed by the peculiarities of each site. Here, the plan for the lower garden below the tennis court was never implemented.

In *The Gardens of Edna Walling* the Durrol design has been described by Peter Watts as being "pure Italianate in concept". Certainly, Miss Walling was fascinated by Italian gardens, and felt that, "the chief elements of the Italian garden — stone, water and trees — are most appropriate to the conditions governing the construction of gardens in Australia". She also wrote often of terracing, another strong characteristic of Italian garden design.

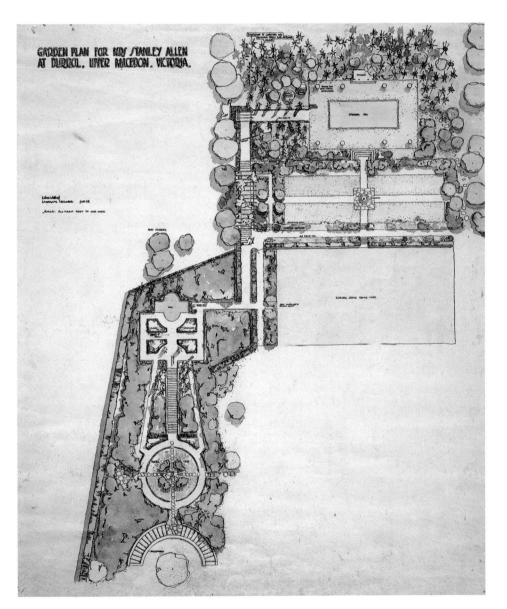

GARDEN PLAN FOR MRS STANLEY ALLEN
AT DURROL, UPPER MACEDON, VICTORIA.

It seems that terraces need to be individual. That is, each one needs to be *different*, different as regards their width, their character and design, and their planting; each an entirely separate garden in fact. Witness the Italian garden composed of terraces. Each terrace is a separate garden; one may be a parterre, one a maze of tall clipped hedges, one a lawn or paved area, and yet another a setting for water features.

Above all pieces of garden construction, terraces are usually referred to with most reverence, and yet so rarely are they sufficiently well disposed and proportioned to warrant such awed tones.

There is nothing more monotonous than a set of stone walls equidistant up and down a hillside; nothing can spoil a hillside more, and there is nothing that exercises the imagination more than working out a garden scheme on a steep slope that looks like a tilted up table!

These concepts were strongly evident in her plan for Durrol. The terraces do, in fact, have different personalities, yet the mature garden is distinctly unified. Each terrace is intimate, secluded and invites a pause, while the perfectly proportioned flights of steps encourage further exploration. Vegetation made lush by the moist and misty climate of the mountain, links each level and adds to the timeless serenity of this very special garden.

□ Behind the sundial the red-brown foliage of an *Enkianthus* blends with the changing hues of deciduous azaleas. Hellebores and grape hyacinths romp in this lush environment.

Cruden Farm

LANGWARRIN
1929

□ Original English elms tower over the circular sweep of gravel in front of the homestead.

Opposite: On a still day, the fragrance from these lemon-scented gums is almost overpowering, an inspired choice by Edna Walling. Underplanted by massed *Watsonias*, these eucalypts provide a surprisingly subtle transition from the simple farm entrance to the elegant home and walled garden.

T he formality of English gardens greatly influenced Edna Walling's early designs. Nowhere is this more evident than at Cruden Farm in Victoria, where the walled garden still stands. This charming stone enclosure, designed sixty years ago to house a rose garden, would appear to be Edna Walling's only remaining walled garden. Complete with elegant wrought-iron gates, it was the major part of her design for the young Mrs Keith Murdoch, now Dame Elizabeth.

Despite the English influence, even at this early stage her gardens almost always included some degree of informality. At Cruden Farm, this is exemplified by the entrance, a meandering avenue of lemon-scented gums lining a simple dirt drive. To blend the formal with the informal, Miss Walling introduced a curved low stone wall to link the driveway to the walled garden.

The simple drive sets off the grandeur of the front entrance and encloses an understated planting of elms and lawn. The gracious house, once a modest farm cottage, was restyled in 1929 by the architect Desborough Annear. Originally, potted bay trees flanked the front door, but this position proved to be too hot, and the one remaining tree was planted in the garden. It is now a huge specimen.

Miss Walling also designed other sections of the garden, most of which were lost in the bushfires of 1944–45 or later incorporated into a different design.

Stone for the walled enclosure came literally from the back garden, and labour was provided by local workers during the Depression. The superb stonework would have impressed Edna Walling, who had very definite ideas on stone construction. Miss Walling believed

. . . that certain ruggedness which makes stone walls beautiful is never to be found in a wall in which tricks have been used to speed its construction, display certain surfaces, or economise on the stone.

The different effects produced by different people using the same stone is sometimes astonishing. A tremendous amount of stonework has been done by "tradesmen" who have no stone sense, and never will have, and many an owner would have done much better himself. It is an art — not a difficult one, but one that demands a love of stone, an appreciation of stone wall building, and a refusal of any temptation to circumvent these traditions by any cheap artifice that may seem a good idea at the time.

Despite the charm of the stonework in the walled garden, the original planting was not such a success. In the Australian climate, the walls created a very hot, damp environment. Black spot was a constant problem in the rose garden, demanding high maintenance, and an avenue of apples, Dame Elizabeth commented, was more conducive to stewed than fresh fruit!

After years of perseverance, Dame Elizabeth elected to change the planting. In the upper walled garden, a herbaceous border now thrives, and the roses have been replaced by a pool. The herbaceous planting in particular suits the proportion of the upper walled garden and is spectacular in summer.

Over the years, Dame Elizabeth, a clever and enthusiastic gardener, has evolved her own special style at Cruden Farm. Using the existing Walling architecture to great advantage, she has created a comprehensive and exciting garden that flows beautifully from the lemon-scented gums of the entrance drive to the massed picking garden.

□ This rare Australian walled garden
typifies Miss Walling's penchant
for formality in her early designs.

Mawarra

MT DANDENONG
1932

□ This statue sits in quiet repose amidst the copse of silver birch.

Opposite: The octagonal pool in the depths of the garden — a place for reflections and reflecting.

*E*dna believed Mawarra to be her finest creation. The scale and sloping site of this garden allowed her to exercise her love of symmetry, architectural construction and grand planting. This lush two-hectare property set high in the Dandenongs remains a superb testimony to her design skills.

Mawarra is not so much a garden as a symphony in steps and beautiful trees.

The site being a steep one, it was decided that the design should consist mainly of a central stairway, terminating in an octagonal reflecting pool.

From the house terrace, one passes down to an oval-shaped terrace where a pool with a bluestone coping is set against the high stone wall supporting the top terrace. The ramp-like steps which are at both ends of the terrace are actually a series of gravel areas sloping to narrow stone steps which are only three inches high, and thus very easily negotiated.

From this lower terrace, to the top of the main stairway a group of long steps connect the walls that come down at either side of the ramp steps. These steps were designed to avoid having a wall at this point. The thirty steps in the main stairway are so easy that one finishes ascending them without exhaustion. The whole arrangement is such that it is hard to realise that one has ascended so steep a slope with so little effort.

The trees are Oaks, Maples and Birches in many varieties seldom seen outside this garden, and they are densely enough planted to give a lovely woodland effect, and in consequence do not look like a collection of horticultural specimens. In the original planting, there were no Blue Spruces, no Golden Cypress, no brilliant masses of Rhododendrons, and no large splashes of bright azaleas. The Rhododendrons and Azaleas are there of course, but planted with restraint, like brilliant jewels in a quiet green setting.

It was never intended that this should be a show garden, but one that would be quietly beautiful, a garden that would weather into greater beauty as the years went on. Maintaining such a garden is such an art, the art of knowing when to leave well alone. ("The Architecture of the Garden", unpublished notes by Edna Walling.)

Designed in 1932 for three sisters, Mrs McMillan and the Misses Marshall, the garden was constructed while they holidayed in England. On their return, the extensive stonework in the then unplanted garden evoked their comment that "it looked like Pentridge Jail".

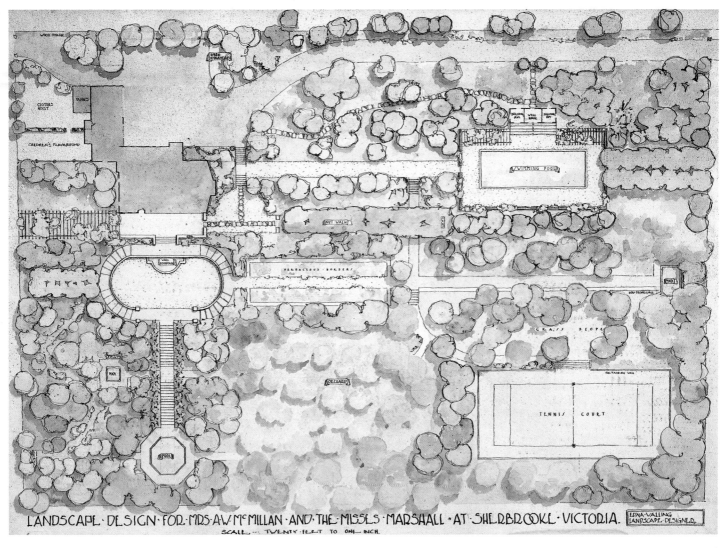

LANDSCAPE·DESIGN·FOR·MRS·A·W·McMILLAN·AND·THE·MISSES·MARSHALL·AT·SHERBROOKE·VICTORIA. | EDNA·VALLING·LANDSCAPE·DESIGNER.
SCALE — TWENTY·FEET·TO·ONE·INCH.

☐ A mossy pathway leads to the charming cottage built as a children's playhouse. A mature tulip tree displays its golden autumn colour, and presides over a weeping elm. In winter the sunlight catches the gnarled branches of the two standard cherries (*Prunus serrulata alba rosea*) enclosed within the gentle curves of the stone ramp.

□ This Dandenong garden of exotics and
magnificent stonework was considered by
Edna Walling to be her finest creation.

This stonework, reputed to have cost
two thousand pounds, provides the key
to the garden's existence — now softened by fifty years of growth.

Despite her passionate involvement
with this garden, Edna Walling walked
off the job following an argument over
money — one pound, in fact. Eric Hammond remained to complete the garden's
construction. Working as landscape contractor with Miss Walling for forty years,
he remembers Mawarra as his favourite
project.

After 1960, when the garden changed
hands, Edna Walling had the opportunity to revisit Mawarra many times
and became firm friends with the owners, Mr and Mrs Frank Walker. In a letter
to a friend, Miss Walling describes Mrs
Walker as "a marvellous gardener"
who had "added with planting quite
beautifully".

Inevitably in a garden of such scale,
massed planting has created dense
shade in once sunny areas.

Moss replaces lawn along shady pathways, perennials such as hellebores and Solomon's seal flourish under the dense canopy, and herbaceous beds have now been replaced by shade-loving shrubs.

Herbaceous borders, which were a constant feature of Miss Walling's early designs, rarely survive today. But at Mawarra, the original herbaceous planting is being re-established in full sun, enabling the Walkers to once again enjoy the pleasure of creating a tapestry of perennials.

Edna Walling has frequently been accused of overplanting. Her instructions, however, to thin out as a garden matured, were rarely followed, probably because her propensity for planting trees and shrubs in groups of two or three often led to a dilemma on the part of the garden owner, who, having become attached to these copses, chose to ignore Miss Walling's well-meant advice.

At Mawarra, the Walkers have chosen to take out the lesser trees where necessary, a difficult task but crucial in such a densely planted aging garden. The removal of one of three mature beech allows sunlight to reflect once more onto the octagonal pool at the foot of the main stairway. The avenue of Italian cypress leading to this pool has been replanted with fastigiate yews which cope better with the shade.

The famous birch copse, which recently fell victim to a fungal disease, has been replaced faithfully and is once again casting dappled shade over the pathway leading to the pool. Edna Walling was adamant that the placement of such trees was never to appear contrived. To achieve this, she would frequently fling a bucket of potatoes and plant a tree where each potato fell. On the arrangement of trees, she wrote:

One day I was summoned to a huge window to admire a new landscape scheme that had been worked out on the distant boundary. The ground was undulating and all about was natural verdure, and there before our gaze stood one row of Lombardy poplars, one row of cryptomerias and one row of Japanese maples. I was unable to speak, and so was treated to a word picture of the scene. It seemed to me like explaining a blackboard with nothing on it! It seems better not to do any planting at all until we can do better than that. But no! With the most amazing confidence trees are assembled, and marshalled on to the landscape much more often in military than in picturesque formation. And yet, when you boil it all down, this landscape gardening business is chiefly a matter of observation. Walk along a country road — one that has not been meddled with, of course — and observe how nature groups her trees and shrubs.

The house at Mawarra now looks into and upon a wonderful blend of towering trees and thick shrubberies. Each of the terraces leading off from the central stairway has a different character and style of planting. Like Durrol, Mawarra shows Miss Walling's leaning towards an Italian influence where the slope of the site is exploited and stone and water play a large part in creating atmosphere.

Endless hours can be spent exploring this garden. Apart from the discovery and appreciation of the original design, there are a multitude of rare and interesting plants to examine, the legacy of the plantswoman who has lived in this garden for nearly thirty years.

□ After the bareness of winter, the exuberant spring growth clothes the stonework in the pastel hues of forget-me-nots, blue bells and cherry blossom.

The Beattie Garden

TOORAK
1 9 3 5

☐ The elegant wrought-iron entrance gate was a collaborative effort between Edna Walling and her friend Jim Beattie. Clipped *Buxus* stand either side of the slate pathway leading to the front door and lower garden. A bronze maiden is glimpsed through a tracery of *Kolkwitzia*.

T he Beattie garden in Toorak evolved from the close friendship between Edna Walling and Mr Jim Beattie and his family. An innovative and interesting man, Mr Beattie had earlier built a thatched cottage as a clubhouse for the nine-hole golf course he had developed at Doncaster. Edna Walling was closely involved and this simple building, without a ceiling and with pine needles for flooring, exemplified her passion for blending architecture into the landscape.

The young Jim Beattie (junior) remembers her penchant for marrying cottages to the earth as "wonderful, except you'd hit your head on the overhanging eaves!".

Sadly, the thatched cottage which brought these interesting talents together no longer stands, but the garden still shows strongly the bones of the design that Miss Walling prepared in 1935 for the Beatties' Toorak home. The classic hand-beaten, wrought-iron entrance gates were, in fact, part of a collaborative effort — inspired by Miss Walling and designed by Mr Beattie. Miss Walling believed that wrought-iron gave "an opportunity of expressing design with a lightness not easily obtained with any other material".

The design for this narrow, steeply sloping site is an example of her aptitude for creating interest in a small area. The smaller the garden, the more she used constructional features to provide a variety of pictures and a sense of mystery. She favoured formal design in small gardens, believing strong architectural "bones" to be more permanently satisfying than mere planting.

The stonework in the Beattie garden, constructed by Ellis Stones, still provides this definite sense of design. A slate path leads from the entrance gate, between clipped *Buxus* and informally planted silver birches, down a flight of stairs to the lower garden. Stepping stones cross the lawn to a small rectangular pool overhung by a huge gingko. Glimpsed through the tracery of foliage at one end of the pool is a demure bust on a pedestal. This lower garden is shady and quiet, totally enclosed by the Chinese elms, hawthorns, lilly pilly, cotoneasters and prunus that effectively screen the boundaries.

Still in the Beattie family, the garden with its enduring design is treasured with other mementoes and memories.

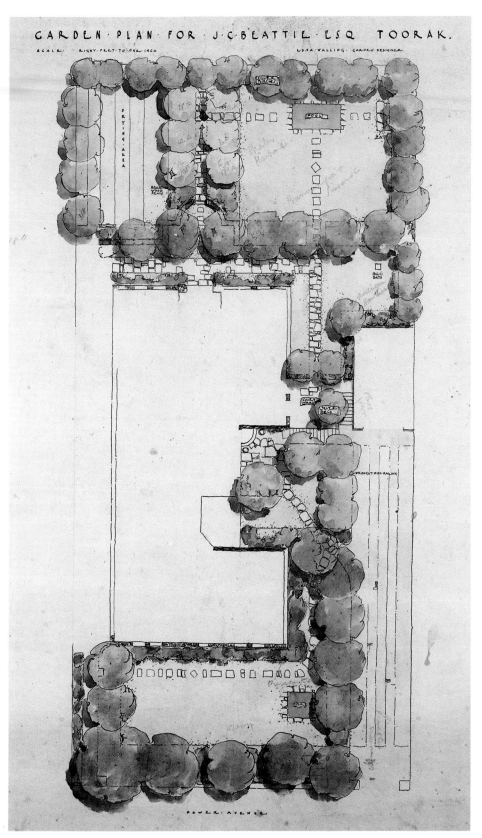

GARDEN PLAN FOR J.C.BEATTIE ESQ TOORAK.

I think the wonderful part about gardening is the fact that there are so many plants that will grow in the most impossible places. I do not mean impossible plants either, but really attractive ones. Take babies' tears for instance (Erigeron mucronatus). It certainly takes possession . . . one man said that he bought a plant for a shilling and now he has a thousand pounds' worth!

☐ Architectural features were an integral
part of Miss Walling's design. Here, a
viburnum and ivy overhang bluestone
and wrought-iron, and a sundial sits in a
tiny paved courtyard.

Ardgartan

BRANXHOLME
1935

□ The unusual outline of the walled rose garden viewed from different aspects.

*T*he unique design of the stone walls at Ardgartan provides the pivot for this garden in the Western District of Victoria. Encircling the formal rose garden, these low walls create a surprising sense of enclosure, while allowing views of the garden and grazing lands beyond. Stone paths crisscross beds filled with roses and add to the symmetry of design typical of the younger Edna Walling. This walled rose garden is one of the few remaining examples of a recurring theme in her early work.

A softer and more spacious sweep of garden envelops this formal section. Always her plans encompassed the simple enjoyment of trees and lawns, as well as more elaborate flower gardens. At Ardgartan, steps lead from the roses down into grassy glades under copses of deciduous trees, and thickets of shrubbery provide a dark backdrop to the sun-dappled lawns. This distinction between formal and informal is definite, yet the skilful design ensures the transition is gentle and well founded.

Elsewhere, further stone walls, less rigidly symmetrical, create a series of secluded "garden rooms". The extensive stonework at Ardgartan, constructed by local Italians with ironstone from the property, remains remarkably intact half a century later.

The preservation of the garden in its original state stems from the strong sense of family history and loyalty that pervades Ardgartan. Five generations of the Youngman family have lived on the property over the past hundred years, and the enthusiasm of the present generation is impressive.

Edna Walling designed this Victorian country garden in 1935 for H. J. Youngman. The Youngman farm diary, straying from its usual pastoral recordings, notes her presence in the garden. An entry on 5 August 1935 reads, "E. W. planting in the garden."

Much of the original planting is still evident. Stately blue delphiniums still line the wall below the drive in summer, a pair of rare *Zelkova* (Japanese elms) turn a soft yellow in autumn, and a huge pin oak dominates the lower garden in all seasons.

Despite the structured formality surrounding the homestead, Ardgartan is essentially a country garden. The property is well known for its Hereford and Corriedale studs and the close affinity between garden and farm is evident.

46

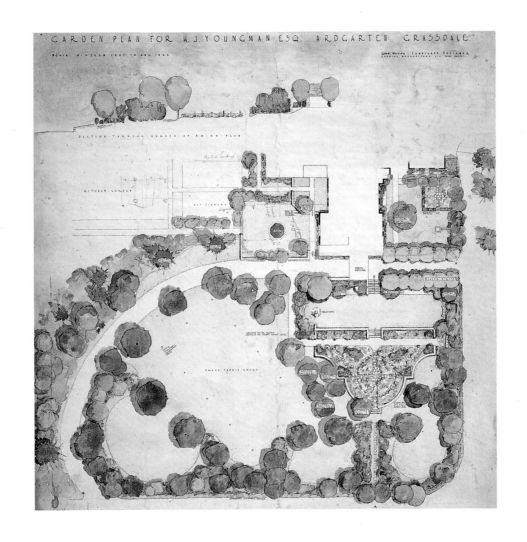

☐ Sensitive planting of valerian, forget-me-nots, daisies and the grey-leaved *Senecio* enhances without masking the rugged stonework of the rose garden.

Below: Beside the house, the only adornment of a simple enclosed lawn is the spring blossom of this pale pink cherry.

The Marshall Garden

HEIDELBERG
1936

□ A rough-hewn wooden bench in a
sheltered circle of lawn is overhung by
Echium, French lavender and
Thryptomene calycina
Opposite: A great friend of the Marshall
family, Edna Walling obviously
influenced the siting and construction of
this timber studio hidden at the bottom of
the garden. Early spring sees the
blossoming of white japonica, *Prunus
mume* and forsythia.

'The close business and personal relationship that existed between Edna Walling and Blanche Marshall led to the design of this appealing garden in Heidelberg, Melbourne. Unique in that Miss Walling was able to have a continuing input into its development over a long period, it remains the most informal of her town gardens.

Blanche Sharpe was a young pharmacist with her own business at Eaglemont when she met Edna Walling in 1926. When she took over the rather haphazardly kept books for this busy landscape designer, they became firm friends. Blanche would often accompany Edna on her rounds of garden visits, and she helped build The Cabin at the bottom of the Sonning garden. In 1928, Blanche paid a hundred pounds for a block of land in Bickleigh Vale. This was to become. The Barn, which she later sold back to Miss Walling. After Blanche's marriage, her family often visited Bickleigh Vale and "Aunty Edna" became godmother to the young Jane Marshall. The Marshall sisters vividly recall the rather avant-garde atmosphere that prevailed in the village. Here, they were introduced to live theatre. The garden at Sonning, with its raised stage and shrubbery wings, provided a romantic backdrop.

The garden Edna Walling designed for the Marshalls was in fitting style for the simple, unostentatious house. There was very little structure — a set of steps, small retaining walls, paths and stepping stones meandering across the grass. All the garden beds curve, and grassy glades disappear around corners. Forget-me-nots, bulbs and hellebores are allowed to define the pleasantly vague edges between garden and lawn.

One always hopes to find a garden full of surprises.

The cottage at the bottom of the garden is a surprise and a delight. No hint is given of this quaint cabin nestling amongst sprays of flowering shrubs, until halfway down the path. Here, the rich brown timber of the cottage with its tiny wooden porch and white windows suddenly creates a charming picture. This studio, used by the Marshall sisters in their youth, clearly shows the influence of Edna Walling. The interior walls demonstrate one of her idiosyncrasies — she always insisted on placing the plasterboard "rough side out".

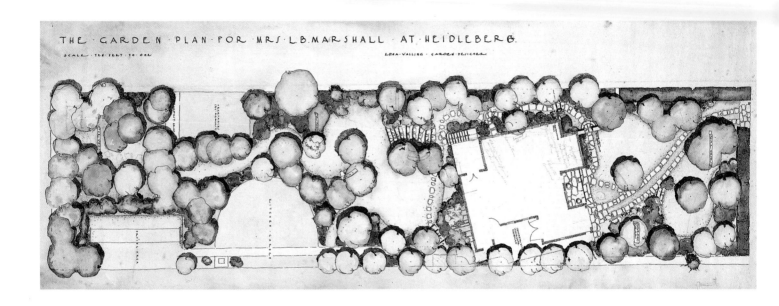

THE GARDEN PLAN FOR MRS L.B.MARSHALL AT HEIDLEBERG.

Mrs Marshall determinedly preserved the informal spirit of the garden and was obviously a great disciple of her friend. Reflecting in *A Gardener's Log*, Miss Walling writes:

I prefer the type of garden where as much permanent ground cover as possible clothes the earth; wherein, when it is once established, a spade rarely appears. Where there are little surprises invented by Nature, patches of self-sown foxgloves, little colonies of alpine violet, which will so obligingly clothe the pathway's edge and run back under the trees and shrubs if encouraged and unrestrained in its wanderings; Columbines coming up in least expected places and many other delights that await the one that gently hand-weeds her garden, steering off all who would help her "clean it up".

This garden, deceptively simple, retained its charm through Mrs Marshall's assiduous "gentle hand-weeding". It has a soft and mellow atmosphere and there is much pleasure in carefully picking a way between overhanging foliage down enticing paths. In this narrow suburban plot, it is still easy to get lost among the forget-me-nots, and to daydream in the sunshine that filters through the graceful foliage of a towering Chinese elm.

After many years of prospering under the one caring hand, this garden has now changed owners. Will it go the way of so many Walling designs and disappear under the "progress" of swimming pool and tennis court, or will it be fortunate and continue to flourish in the midst of another sympathetic family?

□ In this gentlest of town gardens, paths meander among hellebores, freesias and ornamental *Alliums* in early spring (**top right**), while *Prunus mume* overhangs drifts of flag iris yet to bloom.

Silver Birches

BALWYN
1936

☐ At the bottom of the sunken lawn, an informally curved pool provides the major architectural interest in this expansive city garden. Silver birches shelter a large magnolia.

*T*he Silver Birches garden in Toorak is one of the few designs commissioned before a home was built. With great foresight, Mr Douglas George (of Georges Stores in Melbourne) involved Edna Walling in the total concept of home and garden. Instead of fitting garden to house, Miss Walling was able to design the garden as an integral part of the home as she preferred but was rarely able to do. It is thought that she may also have been an influence in the house design, which is unusual. Though a large two-storey home, it is of single-room width, with all rooms featuring spacious windows opening onto each side of the garden.

A magnificent mature oak tree provides an important anchor for the garden which was designed in 1936. As the name suggests, a number of silver birches were planted, most of which have been replaced over the last fifty years.

Although this was a busy stage in her career, Miss Walling spent a year working on the Silver Birches garden, and was responsible for much of the stonework remaining today. In a classic plan complete with slate terrace, low curving stone walls and even a sunken garden, Miss Walling celebrated the use of water by incorporating a pond and a fountain. The pond is situated at the bottom of the garden to draw interest to this area.

Almost scientific in her handling of water features, Miss Walling writes in *A Gardener's Log*:

Pools and other water features have become so popular that no persuasive words are needed to induce owners to install them in their gardens. One or two points not generally known about pools may be of interest here. They need not be deep, eighteen inches or two feet [forty-five to sixty centimetres] being ample, and the presence of mosquitoes will be controlled by the introduction of goldfish. To secure good reflections, and to avoid seeing the sides and bottom of the pool, which is undesirable when they are not tiled, it is necessary to cover concrete with a bitumen paint specially prepared for the purpose; ordinary tar destroys the plant life and kills the fish. Finally, unless it is for a fountain, the basin of which is retained by a moulded coping, the pool should always be, as far as possible, in a position that suggests itself as the most likely place.

If the top of the wall for an informal pool is bevelled back towards the lawn instead of being finished level, the grass will grow right

. . .that little Alyssum "Carpet of snow", is another white flowered treasure I would find it hard to manage without. Although it seeds itself freely it is never a trial in that respect. On the contrary it seems nearly always to come up in the right places, and often in spots where we would never have thought of planting it. These little accidental bits of planting give charm to our gardens more than almost anything else.

to the water's edge. Big flat boulders placed with restraint and artistry can be as delightful as a row of stones can be hideous in the parts where the shrub border butts onto the pool. We may learn much from the Chinese and Japanese in these matters; no other people know the art of placing boulders as they do.

Do your planting on the northern and western sides, so that at the hottest part of the day the pool appears cool and inviting, reflecting the overhanging trees. Low-growing plants of quiet hue, to conceal the edge, will ensure a quiet green and softly textured setting for the pool. Any colour should be most subtly

introduced. Blues and mauves create more distance when looking across the water than brilliant reds, pinks and orange.

In autumn, the water both reflects and provides a resting place for the magnificently coloured exotics in this garden — the richness of the oaks, the translucency of the gingko and silver birches, and the fiery glow of the persimmon. Throughout the year, the pool provides the perfect corner in which to pause for a while and absorb the peace of the garden.

☐ **Above:** White alyssum complements the paper-white of a young cut-leaf birch.

Left: A stone path meanders in the shade of the dense planting behind the pool.

Eurambeen

BEAUFORT
1937

□ A sundial standing amidst rough grass and daffodils, the tracery of grape on old timber beams, and reflections of the pergola in the still waters of the lily pond make this a peaceful and romantic retreat.

*A*n air of establishment, permanence and history pervades the Eurambeen garden and homestead, a feeling that is heightened by the massive spread of the venerable Moreton Bay fig and cypress which tower over the gravel forecourt and garden beyond. These magnificent trees provide a foil for the generous scale of this grand country residence and its surrounding grounds.

A large Western District property, it was settled in 1830, and was once home to the Eurambeen Merino Stud. It now consists of 1620 hectares (four thousand acres) of prime basalt country and runs flock Merinos and Angus cattle. The stone homestead dates from the 1850s. Successive residents have added their own personalities to both home and garden, with most structural additions occurring in the 1920s and '30s.

Edna Walling was commissioned by Mrs Theo Beggs to redesign the garden in 1937. Her fine watercolour plans for the Eurambeen garden showed her ability to take full advantage of existing features and the previous hundred years of growth. The plans showed a simple driveway leading to an expansive gravel forecourt surrounded by a curved stone wall, anchored at each end by the existing fig and cypress. From here, the design became strongly architectural, with large areas of stone paving, and walls and pergola enclosing an existing swimming pool. A second pergola ran down the slope into lawn and generous sweeps of flowers, shrubs and trees. Nearer the house, an intricate network of paths intersected the "spring garden" and small orchard of flowering trees, all enclosed by formal hedges.

In typical Walling style, an area called "the wilderness" offset this formality. A homestead of such stately proportions needed, as a balance, an expansive garden. Her design provided this scale, yet also invited exploration of secluded corners.

The outbreak of war effectively halted any construction, and plans for the lower garden with its grand pergola gave way to the necessity of a vegetable garden. This section was never completed; nor was the formal "spring garden" near the house.

Today, the Walling section is but a part of this large, beautifully maintained country garden. But here the strength of her design is manifest in the ability of her stonework to stand alone, unadorned by any but the simplest of planting.

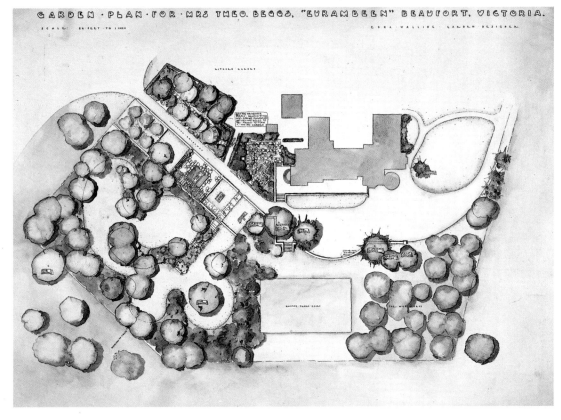

A garden should, I always feel, be just a little too big to keep the whole cultivated, then it has a chance to go a little wild in spots, and make some pictures for you.

□ Century-and-a-half-old trees provided a backdrop for Miss Walling's scheme for this Western District property. Wisteria clambers over timber pergolas, rain glistens on the capping of the superb curved walls of the forecourt, and sunlight streams through an aged cedar.

The Ledger Garden

**BENALLA
1937**

□ A seat in which to pause and ponder.

Opposite: A delicate wrought-iron gate allows a glimpse into this beautifully maintained Benalla garden. From the sun-drenched plane tree, stepping stones lead into the shade of a huge oak at the entrance to the garden.

A treasured note, scrawled in Miss Walling's typically illegible handwriting on a scrap of paper, was found tucked under the front door at Erma and Laurie Ledger's Benalla garden.

"Edna Walling and Ruth Walker called and both decided yours is the best kept garden we have ever seen, everything looks so happy. Very sorry to miss you. We are drifting up to Glenmorgan, Queensland. EW"

Considering the unpromising scene that greeted her on her first visit in 1937, Miss Walling was no doubt delighted by the transformation. On that occasion, she sat on the verandah and looked at the sole contents of the backyard — a poultry run, and clothes line stretching from fence to fence.

"It looks so grim," was her eventual comment.

Undeterred, she produced what the Ledgers describe as, "a most brilliant piece of landscape design". The precious watercolour plan, beautifully framed, is a favourite possession.

Ten years previously, Edna Walling had designed another Benalla garden, for Laurie Ledger's parents. So impressed were the young Ledgers with Yathong, that Miss Walling's expertise was sought when embarking on their own garden.

On this relatively small block, a feeling of spaciousness was created, where sweeping lines of beds lead one on, and vistas are glimpsed through thoughtful

plantings. The constant movement from dappled shade to sunlight and back again adds greatly to the illusion of a far larger garden and to the pleasures of its exploration. There is something very special about patterns of light and shade and the changes of mood they inspire.

Writing in *Gardens in Australia*, Miss Walling says:

There is a mistaken idea that if the area is small it must on no account be broken up for fear it will appear even more limited. The smaller the area the more imperative it becomes to devise some means of making it appear larger. To do this, we must conceal the boundaries as much as possible, and break up the remainder with groups of trees and shrubs which form vistas, creating a sense of distance which does not really exist. The boundary borders may sweep well into the middle of lawn in places, thickly planting these peninsulas with trees and shrubs so that what lies beyond, cannot be seen at once. The reason for the dullness of some gardens is that the whole thing can be seen at

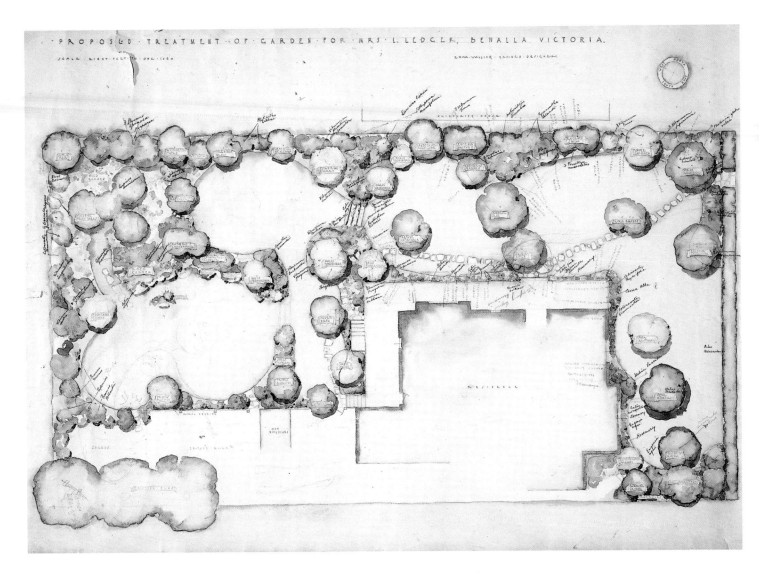

a glance; but for making a closer inspection of some particular bloom, there is no point in walking around it at all.

As one enters through a tall brush fence, stepping stones wander under birches through a shady shrubbery, towards glimpses of sunlight on the grass. Low broad steps lead to a circular lawn, enclosed by thick planting. Paths lead to more sweeps of lawn, Walling-made mushrooms and birdbath emerge from dense ground cover, and a superb gingko, the Ledger's favourite tree, creates another picture.

This creation of "garden pictures" was a signature of Miss Walling's. Through her designs and manuscripts, she encouraged clients and readers to appreciate a subtle planting combination, a focal point at the end of a vista, or a rustic seat in a quiet corner.

In this tradition, the Ledgers have created their own vista of the Benalla Lake, constructed ten years ago. By fashioning a circular opening in the hedge at the bottom of the garden, glimpses of water add another dimension to the design.

Yours is the best-kept garden we have ever seen, everything looks so happy.

As the garden has developed, key views from within the house have been maintained by judicious pruning. This has been skilfully carried out by Mrs Ledger, who has been involved in every facet of the planting of the garden. In gardens nearer to Melbourne, Miss Walling was actively involved in the initial planting, but here Mrs Ledger, with plan in hand, undertook the task herself.

Fifty years of growth have given a maturity to the Ledger garden and the skilfulness of the original design is evident. The Ledgers are one of the few initial owners to still reside in a Walling garden, and their commitment to its care and the preservation of the original design is total.

□ Differing moods are created in this garden by the constant movement from shade into dappled sunlight.
Below: A garden "picture" is created by these Walling-made mushrooms and birdbath underplanted with forget-me-nots and old-fashioned *Aquilegias*.

Boortkoi

□ Even in early spring the herbaceous border along the front façade of the house is massed with the blooms of pink *Silene*, forget-me-nots, cream primroses and babies' tears. This gnarled apple frames the view to the low curved stone wall and paddocks beyond.

Nowhere is the combination of a wild and a formal garden better executed than at Boortkoi, a property in Victoria's Western District. The concept of creating a "wild garden" was much favoured by Edna Walling, and she wrote frequently of the pleasures of uncultivated gardens. This theme is employed on a grand scale and both formal and informal gardens are given equal emphasis in this distinctive garden.

Miss Walling was fortunate to have as a basis for her design, a gracious bluestone homestead overlooking a river. Set amongst a number of mature trees, including a century-old oak and an equally aged olive, the site for the garden commanded fine views of the property.

Commissioned by the then owner, Mr Andrew Manifold, initially, the design for the upper formal garden surrounding the house was carried out. Of the original plan, only the shamrock-shaped flower garden and nearby small rectangular pool were not constructed. The rest, however, was built, and remains largely as designed.

Herbaceous perennial borders still soften the front façade of the homestead, the carefully chosen pastel colour scheme blending subtly with the grey stonework. Babies' tears have seeded with abandon and now soften the paved terrace, which leads onto a simple lawn, enclosed by a semi-circular stone wall.

The rose garden, to one side of the house, is hedged by lavender and backed by a curved stone wall. Flanking the rear of the house, the meticulously maintained gravel entrance area completes the overall impression of thoughtful planting complementing superb design.

This formal garden was completed in 1937 and later in the same year, Andrew Manifold commissioned Miss Walling to design a pergola overlooking the river, as a present for his wife. From this simple request has grown the magnificent "wild garden", which so effectively balances her earlier design.

The planting here is simple. Drifts of daffodils and wild yellow oxalis tumble down the hill under informal plantings of cherry plums, apples, hawthorns and almonds, ending with a huge bank of quinces above the river.

A wide grassy walk leads from the broad stone steps of the upper garden down to simple iron gates opening to paddocks beyond. This bottom corner of the garden, holds charming surprise.

☐ Expansive vistas.

□ Simple cherry plums in the wild garden.

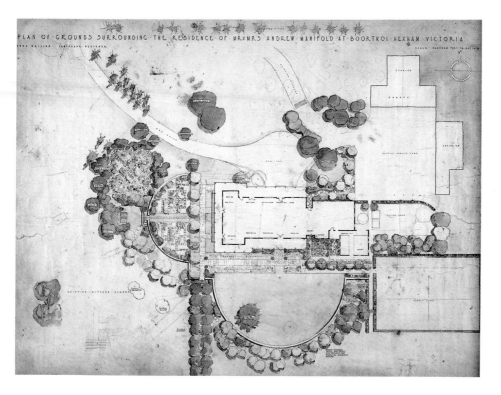

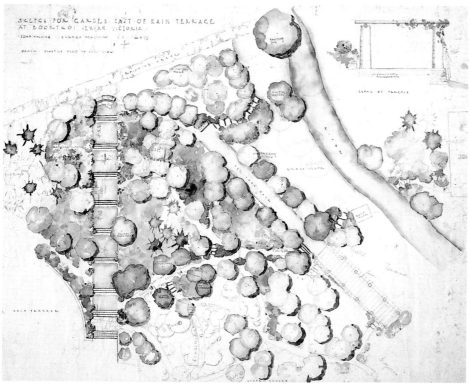

From the bottom of the garden "the long walk" leads through what is perhaps Boortkoi's best known feature, a rough-hewn pergola of ample proportions and rustic simplicity. Hidden from the upper garden, part of its magic lies in the fact that it is so totally unexpected.

An ancient wisteria, originally supported by a farm fence, now clambers over the light sapling beams atop the massive, roughly plastered rubble columns. This generous pergola, approximately thirty metres long and four metres wide (thirty by four yards), is in perfect proportion to the expansive scale of the garden.

Inspired by the famous pergola at Amalfi in Italy, Miss Walling had very definite ideas on the breadth and height these structures should be. Writing in *Gardens of Australia*:

. . . to find oneself in possession of something which was meant to be a pergola that looks more like a monument to a daddy long legs is a little depressing! A low and broad effect is generally safer than anything tall and narrow. There can scarcely be any hard and fast rules about dimensions and proportions, for rarely, if ever, are two sets of conditions alike; so much depends upon the size of the garden, the position the pergola is to occupy, and the architecture of the house . . .

It is fortunate that Miss Walling was requested to enlarge on her original plan, as today the Boortkoi garden stands as a harmonious blend of formal and informal styles. Perhaps one of her greatest remaining legacies, Boortkoi encompasses many of Miss Walling's design principles. No less important is the influence of the present family, who maintain this garden with care and sensitivity.

Low stone walls when simply constructed are always charming. Any elaboration in the form of "tuck pointing" or the use of spectacular stone or even worse, a variety of stones, such as sandstone and marble — to use an exaggerated illustration, gives an eccentric effect.

☐ Majestic elms preside over the enclosed semi-circular lawn in front of the house. In the wild garden below, yellow oxalis and lilies grow unhindered.

The Carnegie Garden

TOORAK
1937

□ A weeping cherry punctuates one of the two herbaceous borders that divide the upper and lower lawns. A russet-toned dogwood contrasts with the dense evergreen boundary planting.

T he late 1930s still saw a strong leaning toward formality of design and structure in Miss Walling's town gardens. Shapes were geometric and symmetrical, while planting was profuse. These gardens always complemented, and were in fine scale and proportion to, the rather grand homes they surrounded. Formal framework and exuberant planting were combined to create differing moods within each garden.

From the shade of its pergola to its sunny terrace, this Toorak garden, designed for Mr and Mrs Douglas Carnegie in 1937, has such varied and enticing corners.

The understated and simply planted forecourt shows the restrained hand of a designer sensitive to the character of this classic home. Two clipped bay trees flank the front door, and mature oaks and Chinese elm cast shadows on the gravel. This elegance is heightened by the subtle colour scheme of green and white.

A black wrought-iron gate designed by the house architect, Tom Freeman, of Yuncken-Freeman, leads into a long, paved and mossy pathway. The planting here is dense and shady, until a break in the foliage opens onto one of the square terraces. Sun streams onto the open lawns and low perennial garden beds that define the boundaries of each terrace.

A rectangular pond is central to the lower terraced lawn, and reflects images of the house amongst the water lilies.

The tall, thick boundary planting begins to create a shady ambience again, as steps lead down to a secluded paved terrace at the bottom of the garden. The mood changes yet again under the extensive pergola, which stretches back to the house. A stone path is crowded by ferns and ivy, and carpeted by fallen wisteria in spring.

Each area in this garden evokes a different response and there is an appreciation of the skill needed to produce this effect in a relatively small space while retaining overall harmony. Subdued colours have created a restful garden, and the preponderance of so much green is refreshing.

Edna Walling often quoted Osbert Sitwell, who believed the secret of some of the world's most beautiful gardens was their restrained use of flowers — "green is the clue to creating a garden, and not the possession of all the hues in the rainbow".

"There is," Miss Walling said, "always the joy of the seasonal high spots provided by blossom and bulbs in spring, for example, hydrangeas in summer, autumn foliage, berries, and chrysanthemums in the fall, but green is of paramount importance...At certain times of the day there is such a diversity of tones among the greens in a well planted landscape garden, that there should be no feeling of monotony, even with no other colour in the garden at the time."

Sophisticated and subtle, this garden has matured gracefully, displaying many of Miss Walling's design principles. With the demise of so many of her creations, this is perhaps the most intact of all her city gardens.

□ Rampant growth of wisteria,
ivy, bamboo and ferns creates
yet another atmosphere.

□ **Opposite:** The classic pool reflects the
stately façade of this Toorak home. The
elegant entrance court has a simple
colour scheme of white and black,
heightened by the deep greens of
clipped bay trees and oaks.

Yarralumla

CANBERRA
c. 1 9 3 8

☐ A forest of trees seen across a broad
sweep of lawn invites exploration.
Opposite: Once inside, shady stone
paths wander amongst massed shrubs
and perennials — gentian blue *Aquilegias*
mingle with forget-me-nots, wisteria, pink
Bellis perennis, spirea and *Viburnum opulus
sterile.*

The Walling garden at Government House is in direct contrast to the grandeur of the surrounding environment. A forest of deciduous and native trees, viewed across the gracious sweeps of lawn and meticulously kept garden beds, invites further exploration. Winding stone paths lead into a shady and hidden world of gentle and contrived untidiness. A soft ambience cloaks this secluded garden, tucked away on the perimeters of the Yarralumla grounds.

Shrubs mass closely amidst drifts of forget-me-nots, bluebells and *Aquilegia*, while trails of wisteria and honeysuckle clamber over any available support. Huge oaks and gums coexist, filtering sunlight to the muted planting at their feet.

The gardens at Government House have been greatly influenced by each successive governor-general, and it was during Lord and Lady Gowrie's residence there, between 1936 and 1945, that Edna Walling was involved.

Despite the aura of splendour that attaches to a viceregal residence, Miss Walling and Lady Gowrie were admirably restrained in their choice of plants. Simple old-fashioned species predominate — hawthorns, spireas, viburnums, laurels and *Berberis* densely screen the boundaries and merge into generous groupings of Japanese anemones, hellebores, day lilies, agapanthus and many different varieties of iris.

Lady Gowrie was known to be an enthusiastic gardener. Interested in developing this area of garden, Lady Gowrie and a friend, Miss Ethel Cummins, carried out the planting together. Very little else is known today of Edna Walling's involvement at Yarralumla, although it is documented that Lady Gowrie visited her at Bickleigh Vale.

In the peace and solitude of this garden, a fountain and statue were later erected in memory of the Gowries' son, who was killed at war.

The enduring, simple design of the Walling section has ensured that this area of the grounds has remained relatively untouched. The thoughtful care and maintenance of planting in the Walling tradition over the past half century clearly illustrates the appreciation and sensitivity of successive incumbents and their gardeners.

The Cuming Garden

TOORAK
1939

☐ Edna Walling's signature plant, the tiny *Erigeron*, clothes these beautifully proportioned curved steps.

Opposite: A carpet of white lawn daisies emphasises the rural charm and simplicity of this Toorak garden.

*T*oorak is an unlikely place to find a rambling country garden. Here, behind a simple dark-green timber fence, lies a Walling garden dating from the 1930s, with all the charm and relaxed air of a rural estate. White lawn daisies carpet the grass like fallen cherry petals, shrubs grow unimpeded by pruning shears, an aged tea-tree fence screens the tennis court, and espaliered fruit trees form a backdrop for the thickly composted vegetable garden.

A towering oak, a present from Dame Nellie Melba in the garden's infancy, presides over the wilder rear garden where Japanese anemone and iris run riot under a spreading witchhazel, *Parrotia persica*, and old-fashioned shrubs jostle hawthorn and crab-apple in a satisfying blend of shapes and textures. Simple brick paving winds past a wooden garden shed to a low stone wall and the orchard beyond.

Architect Marcus Martin, commissioned to remodel the old brick home, was responsible for Edna Walling's involvement in the garden. These two leading professionals had previously worked together on several commissions, including the Toorak residence and garden of Dr Ringland Anderson.

Miss Walling first visited this garden at the request of the Cuming family in 1939. Her immediate reaction was to insist that "all those horrible pollarded oaks will have to be grubbed out". This extensive row of unfortunate trees was removed by Eric Hammond, who remained to construct the stonework.

Designed around the existing trees, Miss Walling's plan incorporated a long herbaceous border, a generous sweep of low stone steps, and several small pools. Sadly, the flower border eventually became too difficult to maintain and was replaced by lawn.

Unlike many Walling gardens, this one was blessed with a sensitive and thoughtful second owner. Edna Walling once again advised, and had the opportunity to guide the growth of one of her earlier designs. A letter written from The Barn, dated 20 July 1960 reads:

First of all I must say how delighted — and relieved — I was to see that so much of the garden still retained the old planting that in its maturity gives the charm that could so easily have been destroyed forever. It now becomes vital that very little is done that is likely to reduce the picturesqueness. In short that when you are in doubt, don't!

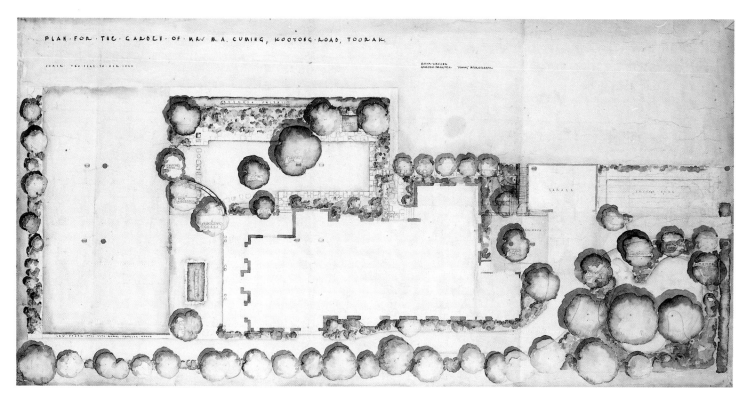

PLAN·FOR·THE·GARDEN·OF·MRS·M.A.·CUMING,·KOOYONG·ROAD,·TOORAK.

I would plant Rosemary and Winter Lavender against the tennis court fence so that it forms an evergreen screen; and back towards the road fence, two or three Italian Honeysuckles (allowed to grow as shrubs that is, not right on the fence). Under that Arizona Cypress (never take this out) Echium candican and Italian lavender. On one of the uprights of Tennis Court fence Evergreen Virginia Creeper.

Replace Hawthorns with Malus ioensis (about three) thus achieving the lovely Spring flowers, pleasant fragrance and Autumn foliage.

That silvery Ivy could be used as ground cover occasionally. In very difficult bare patches *perhaps* a flattish mossy boulder could be slightly sunken in. Very large and very few!

This "picturesqueness" has been judiciously and determinedly maintained. It is not merely by chance that babies' tears smother the stonework and daisies carpet the lawn. It takes a discriminating gardener to enjoy the subtleties of a country garden in the city, and a clever one to know when to "leave well alone".

. . .there was an air of wildness about the garden. It was the sort of garden in which you could garden if you wanted to but if you didn't it would not matter.

□ A classical Walling pool is overhung by a flowering cherry; lavender softens a stone wall; a pathway leads through pink japonica and white lilac; and a rosemary and lavender hedge still borders the original tea-tree fence.

Lavender Lane

FRANKSTON
1942

□ This seaside cottage at Frankston is thought to be the only remaining home designed by Edna Walling outside Bickleigh Vale. Clipped *Buxus* edge one of the many stone paths leading around the house and thickly planted garden. The pergola above the garage, of original design, softens the façade, and the simplicity of this crisp, white cottage remains.

B
est known for her garden designs, Edna Walling also had a flair for the construction of cottages. Frustrated by the mediocrity of the average suburban home, she set about informing the general public of alternatives. *Cottage and Garden in Australia*, published in 1947, was an important vehicle for her ideas. Edna wrote "for those haunted by the dream of a cottage in the country, and also for those already established there, not in attractive cottages, but in rather dull small houses which make no contribution to the landscape and give no particular joy to the owner whose hopes have been suppressed by the inflexible ideas of others."

Lavender Lane remains as the only known example of a Walling-designed cottage outside Bickleigh Vale village. (Lavender bushes spilling over the drive gave the cottage its quaint name.) Edna Walling designed this house and garden for Mrs Veda Timms in the early 1940s at Frankston, Victoria. Aided by Eric Hammond, she was totally involved in the construction of both house and garden.

The cottage is essentially as it appeared in *Cottage and Garden in Australia*, apart from the necessary modernisation of kitchen and laundry. A small bay-windowed room has replaced the northern pergola, adding living area to this typically small two-bedroomed cottage.

The original combination of stone, weatherboard and shingles remains. As at Downderry, the garage is situated under the house, softened by a pergola.

Edna Walling used this technique to "break the abruptness of this particular elevation".

Inside, Mr and Mrs George Walsh, who purchased Lavender Lane from Mrs Timms, have retained the charm of a small English cottage. Moving to Australia from Sussex in 1968, they were immediately engaged by the appeal of Lavender Lane. Mrs Walsh was delighted to learn, three years later, of Edna Walling's involvement in their new home, having spent part of her childhood at Wimbourne in Bickleigh Vale.

Subdivision has reduced the size of the original garden substantially. The initial planting included both natives and exotics, a theme that is continued today. Profusion of growth has been encouraged to protect the cottage from coastal gales. Now hidden from the street, this is a quiet and sheltered refuge.

Kildrummie

HOLBROOK
1948

□ Unusual sculptures seen through eucalypt trunks are a legacy of Margaret Carnegie's art collection.

Opposite: Soft sunlight filters through a spreading ash tree onto the gentle curve of this stone wall.

*T*his Holbrook property's garden, thought to be Edna Walling's first major country commission in New South Wales, was, in fact, her second design for the Carnegie family. Unlike the formal and geometric Toorak garden she designed for them ten years earlier, Kildrummie is based on simple lines. Here, low stone walls, sweeping curves and simple planting illustrate her progression toward greater informality of design as well as her sensitivity to different environments.

At Kildrummie, there is the usual concern for harmony between the low pisé home and its garden. But this is a country property and particular care has been taken to link these agreeably with the surrounding paddocks. Unlike many large country properties where the house and garden are hidden amongst towering English trees, here there are wonderful views of paddocks across low stone walls. The English trees are still present, but in sweeping lines to the side and rear of the garden. Having been allowed to sucker into dense woodland, these elms and poplars screen the farm buildings, shelter the house, and introduce an element of wildness in an otherwise simply planted garden of lawn and trees.

Edna Walling encouraged this type of forest formation, saying it "could be one of the most enchanting features in the landscape treatment of extensive country properties". She went on to say:

Confronted with several acres to be planted, we always seem to be at somewhat of a loss, and frequently end up by dressing up the whole area with specimen trees and lawn, and it is so frightfully dull. To be able to wander off into a little forest somewhere, would be much more romantic, and if we can't be romantic in the development of our gardens, we might as well be dead.

This was one of her first gardens where native trees and shrubs were given an important part in the planting scheme. This planting was supervised by Dulcie and Bernhardt Schubert, early native-plant specialists who no doubt influenced Miss Walling's growing interest in indigenous flora.

Kildrummie was one property where both Edna Walling's key stonemasons, Eric Hammond and Ellis Stones, worked together. True to her tradition of insisting on local materials, all the stone was gathered from the property.

A perfectionist, she chose the largest possible boulders, which were transported with difficulty across the paddocks by tractor and sledge.

Eric Hammond relates how, on occasion, she would order the rebuilding of a stone wall until satisfied with the end result, frequently joining in the heavy labour. She was never one to merely give orders.

Edna Walling designed most frequently for town gardens, and the invitation to work on a large country garden must have always been a welcome change. Confronted with such an expanse, there could also have been the temptation to create *la grande ouvrage*, a temptation that would excite the imaginations of lesser landscape designers. But not Miss Walling, for whom there was always the importance of the site to be considered and its relationship to the environment as a whole; and within that setting, the blending of the home to its surrounding vegetation. She was much more aware of those constraints in the country garden.

Kildrummie bears out her philosophy on simplicity in country gardens, both in concept and maturity.

☐ This is a country garden of sweeping vistas, low stone walls and simple planting.

In the country the restraining hand is imperative if one would preserve the spirit of the garden from anything suggestive of suburbia . . . that the natural grass should roll up to the house on at least two sides is often the most pleasing setting for the country house.

Markdale

BINDA
1 9 4 9

☐ Grape hyacinths and *Kerria japonica* contribute to the rich blues and yellows of early spring.

Opposite: The stylish lines of Professor Wilkinson's architecture are reflected in Edna Walling's lake, simply planted with yellow hot pokers, crab-apples and poplars.

A simple farm gate serves as the entrance to the Ashton property Markdale, at Binda, New South Wales. From the gate, a dirt track winds across the paddocks until a settlement is glimpsed, surrounded by a plantation of poplars, oaks, aspens and elms which have suckered throughout the years into dense thickets. In autumn, the effect is spectacular.

The refreshing simplicity of the approach complements the charm of the turreted homestead and rambling garden. The distinctive architecture of the house was largely the work of the prestigious architect, Professor Leslie Wilkinson. It was he who extended the house into the garden, added a second storey, topped with a copper-roofed cupola, and softened the façade with shutters. The delightful garden was the work of Edna Walling who, utilising the existing trees, created a superb country garden, incorporating stone walls, an extensive pergola, sweeping garden beds, and a peaceful stretch of water in view of the house.

The original holding dates from 1836 and was taken up by the Ashton family in 1921. Mr James Ashton, who built the central part of the present homestead, was at one time the minister of lands. One of his four sons, Mr Geoff Ashton, and his late wife Janet, were responsible for the remodelling of both home and garden.

Miss Walling began work on the garden in 1949, bringing many trees from her nursery at Sonning. Mrs Ashton was also involved in the planting scheme. The magnificent stonework was constructed of local granite and supervised by Eric Hammond, who travelled weekly from Victoria to this property near Crookwell.

Markdale must have been a favourite garden of Miss Walling's, for she commented in a letter to a friend, Mervyn Davis, that it was "one of the most interesting jobs". In another letter to Miss Davis, in 1965, Miss Walling wrote of her contribution to this garden.

The best thing I did there was to deal with the erosion in the paddock over which I was taken for a walk one Sunday morning. It was within view of the living room windows... "Why not dam it back and have a lake?" I sez! and in consequence this stretch of water is the principle feature of their landscape seen over and beyond my low stone wall...we pushed the drive around (in no time with a

The merest trickle of a stream may be dammed back to produce a lake sufficient in extent to accommodate a boat, and as the Water Rat remarked to Mole, "Believe me, my young friend, there is nothing — *absolutely* nothing — *half so much worth doing as simply messing about in boats."*

bulldozer) to the other side of the house. I like to think that those two jobs made it worthwhile to pay me.

Pools were a constant feature of her designs, but here at Markdale she was able to create a generous expanse of water in keeping with the style and scale of the garden. A path winds around the edge of the dam amongst the poplars and flowering crab-apples. On a still day a perfect image of the gracious homestead is reflected in the water.

Markdale is a comprehensive garden. The generously proportioned timber pergola that gently steps down to the tennis court provides a major axis. Large sweeps of herbaceous and shrub beds create enclosed areas of fine lawns within their curves. Low stone walls and informal hedges of spireas and dogwood echo these curves and mark the boundaries between the cultivated and the uncultivated. Below the walls, rough-mown grass massed with daffodils leads to the dam. A garden of this scale and character needs a unifying influence. Restrained planting provides this link — huge drifts of snow in summer, shasta daisies, white ranunculus, viburnums and spireas create a preponderance of white, while love in the mist, forget-me-nots and grape hyacinths weave a soft blue into the tapestry.

As with other country properties she designed, Miss Walling took full advantage of "borrowed landscapes" wherever possible. Thick boundary planting was implemented only for screening and shelter purposes, leaving open beautiful vistas across paddocks and hills. The Ashton family have the combined pleasures of enjoying flowers on their doorstep, a backdrop of superb deciduous trees, and views of distant countryside.

☐ Views of this extensive country
garden illustrate the many moods
created by Miss Walling's design.

Naringal

CAPE CLEAR
1951

☐ Softening the base of the curved wall bordering the forecourt are *Felicia, Arctotheca* and blue ranunculus.

Opposite: Massed drifts of hellebores and sheets of forget-me-nots densely clothe the ground beneath deciduous trees.

N aringal is one of eight pioneer properties in Victoria settled prior to 1845 and still owned by its original family. There are presently three generations of the Rowe family living at Naringal, the youngest being the sixth. The first settler, William Rowe, who selected Naringal in 1841, is buried in the private family cemetery. Recently classified by the National Trust, it is one of the few still in use in Victoria.

Situated in the Western District, Naringal is a grazing property of more than two thousand hectares (five thousand acres), running Merino sheep, Hereford cattle and Cashmere goats. Much of the property was burnt in the disastrous bushfires of 1944, including the original Victorian homestead and garden.

Rebuilding was delayed until after the war when, in 1945, one wing of the house was resurrected. At this time a cousin of the family had studied at Burnley Horticultural College with Edna Walling and suggested that she recreate the garden.

Mrs Rowe remembers Miss Walling moving *everything*: "If she could have moved the house six inches — she would have!"

The design completed, a landscape construction team descended upon Naringal. Moving into the shearers' quarters, complete with cook, they worked solidly for nine months, and totally disregarded inclement weather. Once again, Eric Hammond supervised all the stonework and Miss Walling returned at intervals to monitor the progress of the garden's growth. Their combined skills are seen in the low stone wall surrounding the entrance area, now almost a leitmotif of Miss Walling. Restraint in planting is evident. A single purple-leaf birch marks the front door, while mauve wisteria softens the house façade. Below the stone wall, a generous herbaceous and shrub border, predominantly in blues and pinks, has been planted.

The original, ambitious plan incorporated a tennis court, herbaceous borders, stone walls, mass planting of both natives and exotics, and a swimming pool. It also intended that heavy tree planting including groups of linden trees, red maples, hornbeams, English and American ash and birches, would be used to soften the pool. Miss Walling envisaged that the pool would be painted

black to better reflect the changing leaf patterns throughout the seasons, a startling concept at the time. The idea seemed too impractical and was never carried to completion.

While delighted with the architectural design of the garden, the Rowes nevertheless felt that some of the massed planting schemes would eliminate favoured views of their property. As a result, much of the planting illustrated on Miss Walling's plan was not undertaken.

I often wonder why some people do not regard white as a **bright** *colour; actually, it's the brightest colour in the garden on a moonlight night, a heaven sent blessing to all who would make photographic records of their gardens, and a perennial delight to those who like restful, cool and quiet effects.*

□ Stepping stones lead through hellebores into the white garden, an area originally designated for herbaceous perennials and fruit trees.

Elizabeth Rowe has initiated new gardening schemes around the original plan. Her white garden, an inspiration from Sissinghurst, would surely have had Miss Walling's full approval.

Today, although the bones of the garden are distinctly Edna Walling, the planting owes much to Elizabeth Rowe. She has managed skilfully to blend her ideas with those of the original designer.

☐ A visit to Sissinghurst inspired the preponderance of white. Flowering here are white delphiniums, daisies, candytuft, and blue and white borage.

Kiloren

CROOKWELL
1951

□ Sunlight streams through the early morning mist enveloping the single radiata pine that anchors the garden.
Opposite: A soft coating of snow gives a fairytale look to the Kiloren garden.

"Crookwell is the coldest place on earth," Miss Walling was heard to mutter on her return to more temperate Mooroolbark. Nevertheless, after designing nearby Markdale for the Ashton family in the late 1940s, she returned to this small country town on the Southern Tablelands of New South Wales to create a garden for Dr and Mrs Broadbent.

Kiloren is a garden of exotics. Despite Edna's move toward native planting schemes in the '50s, this frosty high-altitude garden lent itself to an English style of planting. While deciduous trees thrive and colour spectacularly and perennials flourish, only a limited range of cultivated natives survive the low temperatures of this region.

In 1951, the sole tree on this bare, windswept hillside was a *Pinus radiata*. Now sheltered and tranquil, the garden nestles amongst copses of mature trees. Large sweeps of lawn lead into grassy glades carpeted with golden leaves in autumn; light and shade pattern the pathway under the pergola leading to the sun-drenched courtyard; and forget-me-nots appear in every available niche.

Edna Walling loved the challenge of undulating sites and wrote frequently about the interest of changes in level:

How important it is to take advantage of anything unusual about the site, and to guard it against any interference...such raised pieces of ground may be used with great effect in screening off some other part of the garden, so that the whole is not seen at a glance, and the planting...becomes more quickly effective.

This sloping one-and-a-quarter-hectare (three acre) garden gave Miss Walling scope to construct dry stone retaining walls and steps and so make the most of these changes in level. The mound of earth from the house excavation was enthusiastically exploited and as she predicted, has become one of the most successful parts of the garden. Planted solely with natives according to her wishes, very few of these original plants survived. Today, brooms and ground covers mingle informally with the remaining hardy grevilleas, and the mound creates a natural division between grassy woodland and more formally planted garden beds.

Hawthorn laden with bloom at the moment, my thoughts are always of the luscious meadows of England, and a peacefulness pervades the mind.

Miss Walling returned to this garden on several occasions. The Broadbents recall her propensity for physical labour — "working like a galley slave all day" — and the rapidity with which she would decide on a particular aspect of design. Miss Walling and the house architect worked simultaneously on this property and the latter, a man respected in his profession, was apparently subject to much direct comment. As Mrs Broadbent remembers, Miss Walling was almost always correct and usually had her way!

Edna Walling's writings have been a professed inspiration to each gardener at Kiloren. Her ability to communicate so effectively and descriptively her gardening philosophies, will continue to play a large part in its development and maturity.

One of her later designs, Kiloren is less than forty years old and is therefore a relatively young garden in Walling terms. Much of the original planting is just reaching maturity, while still retaining a certain freshness. Italian lavender, babies' tears and Westmoreland thyme colonise stone walls, and multi-stemmed silver birches and hawthorns are an important part of the larger scale planting.

Miss Walling loved the *Crataegus* tribe, and ornamental hawthorns play an important part in the backbone planting of this garden. At any time in autumn, there are yellow, red and orange berries amidst the superb leaf colouring of these trees. In late spring, they are a mass of simple white blossom, and in winter their twisted, twiggy branches throw rugged outlines against clear blue skies. Their absolute hardiness and sculptural habits of growth endear them to lovers of country gardens, where they have space to flourish naturally. For Edna Walling they were also a reminder of her birthplace.

What an atmosphere of rural restfulness these Hawthorns give to a garden! It is, perhaps, that they remind us of the quiet English countryside. When I awake in the morning and look out upon the double pink

☐ Leitmotifs of Edna Walling — Italian lavender, Westmoreland thyme and *Erigeron* spill over a dry-built retaining wall; multi-stemmed birches rise out of a drift of *Phuopsis stylosa*.

□ Yellow forsythia and prunus bloom in early spring
on the hillside above the house. Blooms flower
profusely on the mound; fallen leaves of
golden elm, lime and oak in the woodland;
a *Virburnum burkwoodii* turns
rusty red in autumn.

The Freiberg Garden

KEW
1 9 6 0

□ This Australian native garden complements the lofty modern house, both unusual in their time. Bluestone walls constructed by Eric Hammond provide the architectural "bones" of this informal garden.

W hile Edna Walling had frequently used and written enthusiastically about native plants, they were always of minor importance in her planting schemes. By the 1950s, her growing respect for native flora was reflected in designs, which, increasingly informal, now emphatically favoured native plantings.

In the traditional Melbourne suburb of Kew, a startlingly modern house on a steeply sloping site provided the canvas for a Walling-designed bush garden. In 1960, Michael and Freda Freiberg had commissioned architect David Chancellor to design their house. To design the garden, he recommended Edna Walling, at that time unknown to the Freibergs.

With four young children to claim her time, Freda was looking for a low-maintenance garden. Miss Walling's suggestion of a totally native garden was at that time considered quite avant-garde. The concept of low key, natural planting married well with the architecture of the house. The usual Victorian-era garden of exotics would not have complemented this innovative building so cleverly as the quiet colours and relaxed form of Australian natives.

Such a steeply sloping site, unusual for Melbourne, demanded skilful design. Construction of the bluestone retaining walls and steps was equally crucial. This was one native garden in which rock outcrops were considered unsuitable, and the final design resulted in an interesting blend of indigenous flora and dressed stonework. Eric Hammond, then in his sixties but still working with Miss Walling, provided the necessary expertise. The planting scheme was devised and carried out by a young designer, Glen Wilson, who had previously studied under Miss Walling.

Every plant was selected and placed for the particular purpose of screening the boundaries. This screen worked most effectively when the garden was eight to fifteen years old. Almost three decades on, the eucalypts have matured and no longer provide an effective barrier, which has necessitated underplanting. The towering gums, however, now complement the scale of the lofty building. The height of the house allows close appreciation of these eucalypts. Clusters of softly patterned trunks fill the view from every window, and the fragrant foliage of a magnificent lemon-scented gum reaches into the upper balcony.

The Stewart Garden

TOORAK
1963

□ *Campanula poscharsyana* clothes the base
of a marble pedestal.

Opposite: The gentle greys of lamb's
ears, catmint and English lavender spill
onto the gravel drive.

The Stewart garden in Kenley Court, Toorak, is thought to be Edna Walling's most contemporary remaining garden. Designed in 1963, this garden shows a return to traditional plantings, which was a reverse of the trend toward native landscapes favoured late in her career. Lavender hedges, silver birches, formal slate terrace and marble pedestal intimate her underlying love of "romantic" gardens, and show once again her innate ability to provide a plan in harmony with home and owner. A garden of natives in this setting would have been incongruous.

An elegant two-storey home in one of Melbourne's fashionable inner suburbs, it is beautifully complemented by the simple yet serene garden. The entrance court incorporates an informal pool set amongst craggy boulders in a greenery of water iris and swathes of Japanese windflower, lightly shaded by silver birches. A generous white gravel driveway is lined with lavenders, lamb's ear, babies' tears and catmint.

On the other side of the house, a modest front garden provides serenity and seclusion. Formal stepping stones lead from a colonnaded terrace across lawn to a paved area shaded by a magnificent silver birch and scattered with Walling-made pots. Each one unique, these pots, on Miss Walling's advice, have been left empty and provide just the perfect touch of artifact in the garden. The planting is simple, with green the predominant colour. Silver birches are planted singly in the lawn, which is bordered by thick boundary shrubbery. A walkway of French lavender is still used for drying handkerchiefs and provides a touch of old-worldliness.

When designing a garden Miss Walling's plans always went beyond merely providing a planting scheme, and here her advice to replace the cement terrace with slate and incorporate generous slate steps has transformed the front of the house. It was her unique eye for detail that gave a Walling garden that certain air. In one of the many letters between Miss Walling and Mrs Stewart, she mentions such finer points as painting a window ledge — "Yes I think that window ledge would be better painted charcoal grey and underneath it perhaps plant Erica Darleyensis right along" — and the marble pillar tucked away in a corner of the garden — "Somewhere in *Gardens of Australia* you will find a head

104

of Beethoven, that's the sort of thing I had in mind for that pillar''.

Miss Walling's "landscaping" also went beyond the boundaries of the gardens she designed. In another letter to Mrs Stewart she wrote: "Perhaps you could persuade the owners of the land where the flats might go to plant White Peppermints (*Eucalyptus linearis*) or the Melaleuca the Cumings used...see that Jasminum polyanthum covers their eastern fence."

The chief request made by
...the owner of Lynton Lee
ran something like this:
"I simply must have some
lavender bushes on which to
dry my handkerchiefs."

There was much correspondence between Miss Walling and Mrs Stewart. Edna Walling had actually designed three gardens for Mrs Stewart (who was then Mrs Bill Morgan) and advised on two country retreats. The letters are perfectly characteristic of Miss Walling — often illegible, after-thoughts scrawled in pencil on any available space on the page, frequently undated, and clearly the work of a busy person who wrote as thoughts tumbled through her mind.

Her generous character is portrayed in one snippet — "for that narrow border below the paved terrace, you had better come up and collect bits of the thyme I have here". Later, she writes from Bendles in Queensland, "One of the pleasant things about my departure is that some of the things I treasure have gone to *your* garden, and I am glad too that it is a little garden that I am really pleased with."

Beside her folder of letters from Miss Walling, Mrs Stewart has many tangible memories of this talented woman. She speaks of her unconventional use of trees and shrubs as "nurse" plants. She would advise planting a buddleia or even a flowering almond to provide shelter to more delicate plants with the command: "Remove it after one year — it will have performed its help and will cost less than a bunch of flowers." Mrs Stewart firmly believes this practice led to a misconception that Edna Walling overplanted — few gardeners were disciplined enough to remove these nurse plants. She also speaks of Miss Walling's planting technique for trees in a copse. Having flung a bucket of potatoes, "she would literally stand over you to make sure each stake was placed in *exactly* the position of each potato".

The Walling spirit is evident in this Melbourne town garden, and is maintained by the guiding hand of the Stewarts' gardener, Robert Grant, who worked for many years with Ellis Stones and knew Edna Walling. The collaboration between Mrs Stewart and Robert Grant has ensured the garden's quiet repose and gradual development into maturity.

□ A quiet pool creates a tranquil atmosphere in the entrance forecourt; white and French lavenders, shasta daisies, pink centaurea and the low-growing *Felicia* provide a lesson in harmonious planting; handkerchiefs are still dried on the hedges of French lavender by the wood shed; a mature cut-leaf birch filters sunlight into the living rooms.

Wairere Restoration

MANSFIELD
1925

Wairere was reputed to be Edna Walling's first country garden. The plan for this Mansfield property was published in *Australian Home Beautiful*, 12 February 1926, and was one of her earliest articles for this magazine. An ambitious plan covering one and a quarter hectares (three acres), containing intricate formal herbaceous borders and pergolas, it nonetheless retains the feel of a large country garden.

The garden was designed for Major and Mrs Rutledge, and their daughter, now Mrs Weatherly, remembers vividly its making. Edna Walling lived with the family for three months while tackling the huge task of building every stone wall and laying every pathway. Her enthusiasm obviously knew no bounds, as in the course of construction she added a circular, sunken rose garden, a hazelnut walk, an iris garden and a number of trellises.

"There were two pergolas and three long trellises. She had a passion for wichuriana roses and wisteria mixed together and I will never forget trying to prune them. I have never planted a wichuriana rose since…It was an appallingly labour-intensive garden as my mother and I discovered when our gardener joined the army in 1940," Mrs Weatherly recalls. Despite the wichurianas, gardening has been a life-long passion.

As a child, Mrs Weatherly trailed after Miss Walling until they made together a garden under the nursery window full of wallflowers. Later, there were family picnics at nearby Eildon Weir, digging up bulbs from the deserted gardens.

The garden surrounded a rambling country homestead which was burnt to the ground in 1942. The property was later resumed for soldier settlement and a new house built on the original site. "In the inimitable way of the Soldier Settlement Commission they made the garden the boundary of two farms and gave the major water supply to the very old cottage on the place with no garden," according to a letter from Mrs Weatherly.

After the departure of the Rutledge family, Wairere fell into disrepair. The trees in the garden and the shrubberies bordering the drive continued to grow, while the flowerbeds and stonework disappeared under layers of grass and weeds. Wairere was inhabited, yet the garden languished.

In 1982, Wairere was rescued and its old garden is now re-emerging under the enthusiastic care of the fourth owners. Maurie and Trish Bull are energetically restoring this once magnificent garden according to its original concept. With no prior knowledge of the garden's history or of Edna Walling, they were nevertheless aware of the garden's potential — towering trees, unusual shrubs and the constant discovery of new plants pushing up amongst the blackberries as the seasons progressed.

Countless stone paths have been unearthed. The first hint of submerged stonework was often the lawnmower blades making contact with rock. Further exploration revealed a pattern to the stonework, and eventually an exciting network of paths and walls emerged.

Aged wisterias and rambling roses that had sprawled for many years without support are now clambering over new wooden pergolas. The outside reading nook, a stone seat sheltered by a rose arbour, is once again an enticing retreat. Herbaceous perennials now fill the garden beds near the house and the overgrown privet hedge lining the drive has been trimmed to its original height. The thrill of rediscovering Miss Walling's plan in 1987 has added another dimension to the challenge of restoring the garden as honestly as possible.

In many tangible and intangible ways, Edna Walling has touched on the lives of the new residents of Wairere. Endless hours of physical labour and embracing of new philosophies has led an unsuspecting couple from a tumbledown garden to the recreation of a landscaper's dream.

A little track running through trees and shrubs to no one knows where; little paths that may be just of earth or just sprinkled with gritty sand or inconspicuous gravel are very fascinating.

□ **Far left:** The transformation of the hazelnut walk within three seasons.

Far right: Wisteria and climbing roses are once again supported by timber pergolas.

Left: The wichuriano roses waiting for the reading nook to be reconstructed.

Fragments of Design

Retracing the steps of such an active woman led down many exciting pathways — some proved to be dead ends, some glimpses into forgotten gardens, and some brought rewarding discoveries.

Stumbling onto shady pools choked with vegetation and unearthing overgrown stone walls tucked in the corners of suburbia led to a photographic collection of garden fragments. As the vast network of her creations was discovered, it became fascinating and compelling to trace this woman across so many miles, and to appreciate more and more the extent of her influence.

So, although merely remnants, this collection still provides valuable insights into the Walling tradition of garden design and is an important contribution to this contemporary record.

☐ Designed in 1930 for Miss Isobel Burdett, a Collins Street chiropodist, this was always a holiday retreat. Set within a 1.3 hectare (3¼ acre) block, the plan (page 132) incorporated an extensive pergola, an octogonal herbaceous garden and circular enclosed lawn, seen opposite.

☐ French lavender still graces the
stately cloumns of this Benalla
home. Edna Walling designed this
once extensive garden for
Mrs H. Ledger in 1928. (See plan,
page 131.)

□ This wonderfully designed garden on the banks of the Yarra at Eltham survived in its original form until bushfires raged through the area in 1964, destroying all but the large trees. Commissioned by Mr G. Petre, it once incorporated an extensive pergola, circular rose garden, formal herbaceous garden and a walk of flowering crab-apples. It was rediscovered by earlier owners in 1968 who were enchanted by its wildness. The remaining fragments are treasured. (See plan, page 132.)

The Garden Plan for Mrs Ringland Anderson, Toorak.

☐ A collaboration in 1934 of architect Marcus Martin, landscape designer Edna Walling and owner Mrs Ringland Anderson was the beginning of Chierston — a Toorak estate of magnificent proportions. The garden originally incorporated twin herbaceous borders, a wild garden and one of Melbourne's earliest swimming pools. In the garden's prime, one of its many prestigious visitors, Sir Francis Roland, commented to Mrs Anderson: ''Mary, I hope you won't be disappointed in heaven.'' Remaining are the elegant wrought-iron entrance gates, steps and the stylish pergolas bordering the swimming pool.

☐ Designed in 1936 for Sir Clive and
Lady Steele, this small Toorak garden
complements the two-storey
American-style house. Eric
Hammond constructed the stone
walls and paving around the giant Pin
oak that anchors the garden.

Have you ever noticed how a garden that needs very little attention is so often much more charming and restful than one in which much labour is expended on its upkeep?

□ This Monaro homestead still retains its elegant façade due to Edna Walling's intervention. Visiting to advise on the garden, she arrived in time to prevent the entire verandah being removed from this large country home. Miss Walling sited a low curved stone wall now softened by drifts of flag iris.

119

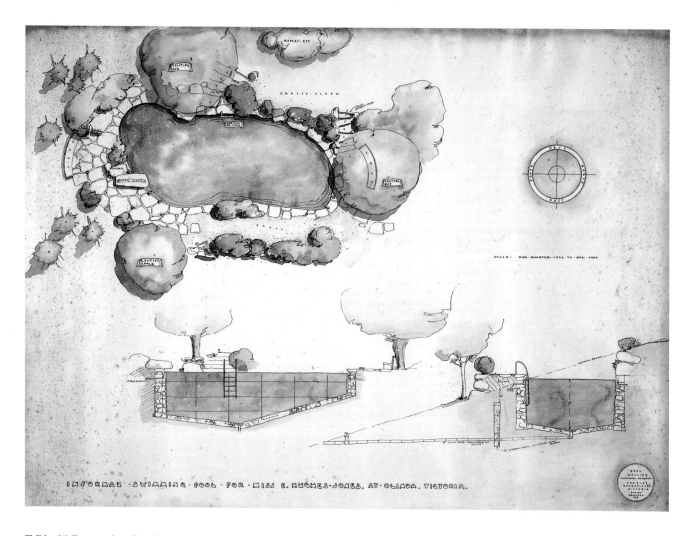

INFORMAL·SWIMMING·POOL·FOR·MISS·E·HUGHES-JONES, AT·OLINDA, VICTORIA.

□ Edna Walling was thought to have designed this garden as early as the 1920s and today wonderful remnants of stonework and terracing remain amidst the abundant Mt Dandenong growth.

☐ This natural bushland swimming pool was perhaps the earliest of its kind. Designed in 1939 for Miss E. Hughes-Jones and constructed by Ellis Stones, it was hidden at the foot of a huge rambling garden.

□ The Oak Hill garden at Ferntree Gully was designed for Dr Farrow. The intricate plan copes well with the steeply sloping site and includes extensive stonework, formal rose garden, large kitchen garden, small orchard and wild garden.

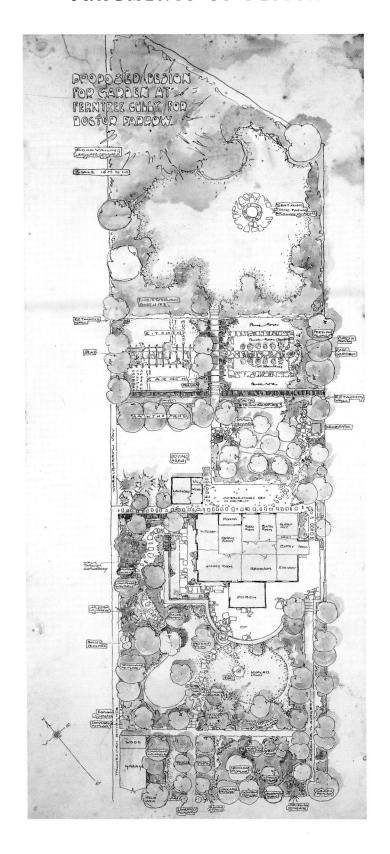

Really, for gate-crashing commend me to Foxgloves! They just make up their minds and off they go to some spot in the garden, perhaps to some corner you have not had time to think about (and how one loves them for that alone), or perhaps into a border where you had quite different ideas.

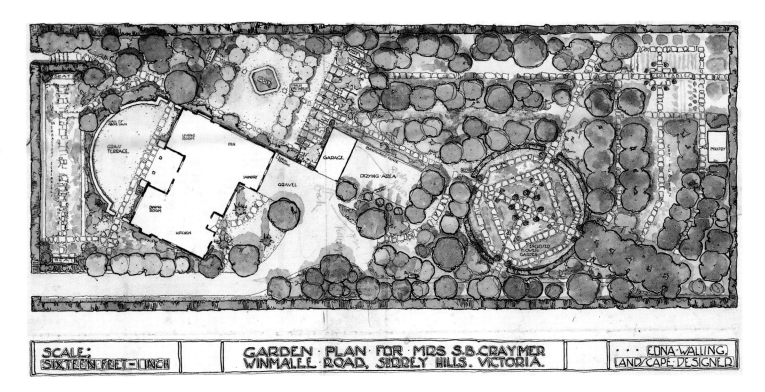

SCALE; SIXTEEN FEET = 1 INCH

GARDEN · PLAN · FOR · MRS · S.B. CRAYMER · WINMALEE · ROAD, SURREY HILLS. VICTORIA.

· · · EDNA WALLING · LANDSCAPE DESIGNER

☐ Designed for Mrs S. B. Craymer of Melbourne, all that remains of this superbly detailed plan is the grassed terrace enclosed by a semi-circular stone wall and twin herbaceous borders at the front of the house.

☐ Miss Walling first visited Port Kembla No. 2 Colliery in 1948
at the request of Broken Hill Associated Smelters. High on this
rainforest escarpment are a group of company homes beautifully sited
by Miss Walling and surrounded by restful plantings of
greens and whites. She was delighted with the chance to utilise
coalmining machinery to place huge boulders.

☐ Eric Hammond worked with Edna Walling for forty years
and was responsible for most of the superb stonework in her gardens.
This design for his garden at the rear of the house once incorporated
a long pergola dividing double herbaceous borders. Stepping
stones still lead through twin silver birches to a quiet mossy pool.
(See plan, page 133.)

□ Penny Green Garden was an early design for Miss Jessie Cook, a kindly English gentlewoman of independent means who used this as her retreat from her Toorak home. Her love of natives led her to plant roadside eucalypts in the Bayswater area. The tiny remaining fragments in this now subdivided garden are the overgrown pool and stonework smothered in charming white oxalis.

Garden Plans

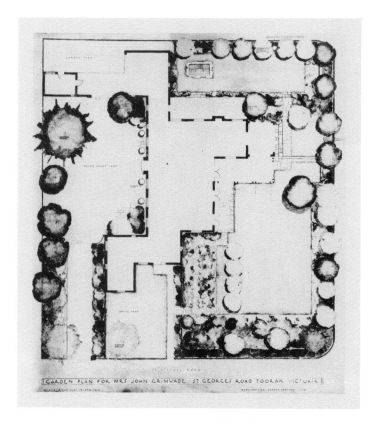

GRIMWADE GARDEN
TOORAK

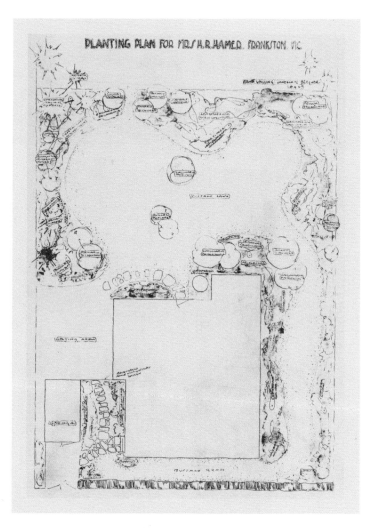

GULLS WAY
FRANKSTON

GARDENS PLANS

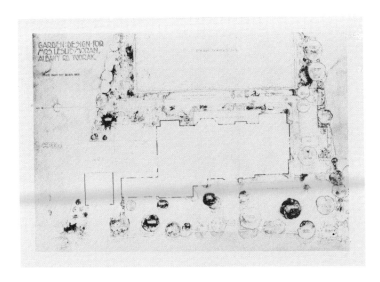

LITTLE MILTON
TOORAK

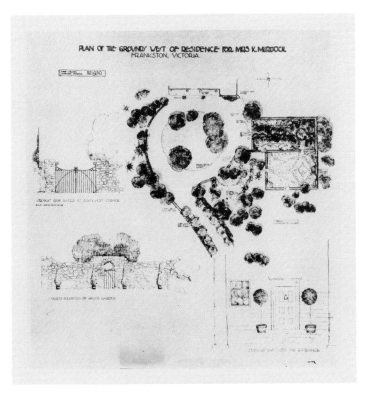

CRUDEN FARM
LANGWARRIN

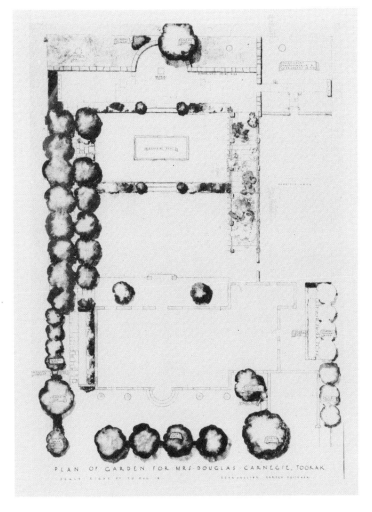

THE CARNEGIE GARDEN
TOORAK

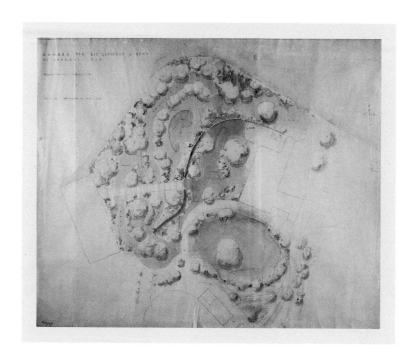

MARKDALE
BINDA

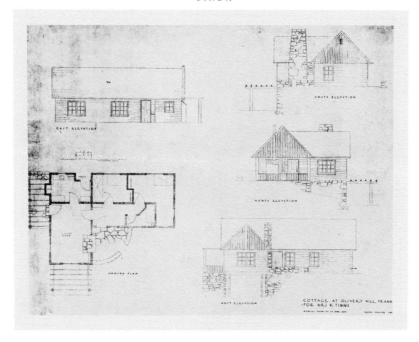

LAVENDER LANE
FRANKSTON

GARDEN PLANS

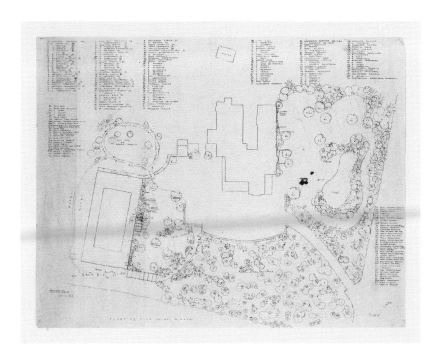

NARINGAL
CAPE CLEAR

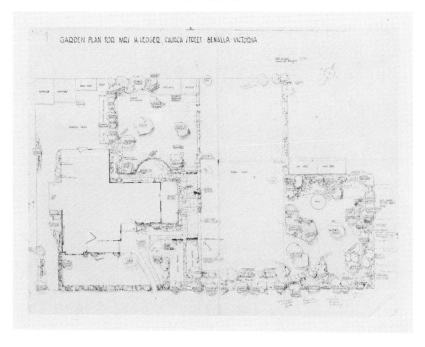

YATHONG
BENALLA

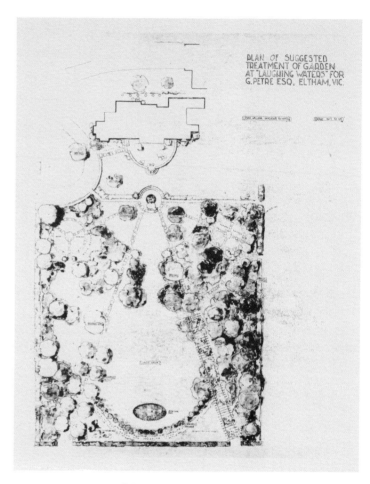

BURDETT GARDEN
LILYDALE

LAUGHING WATERS
ELTHAM

GARDEN PLANS

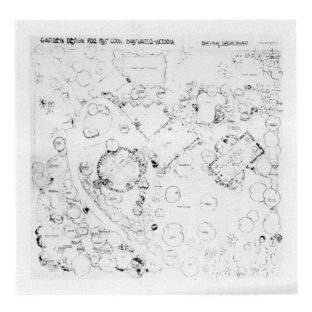

COOK GARDEN
BORONIA

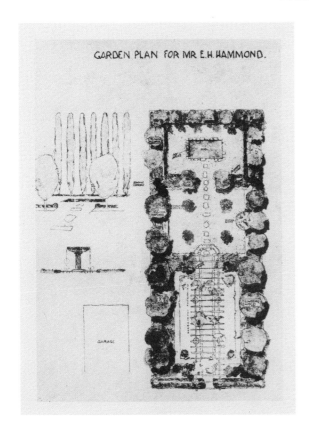

HAMMOND GARDEN
BOX HILL

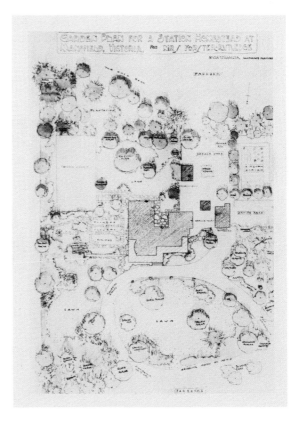

WAIRERE
MANSFIELD

BIBLIOGRAPHY
and other sources

Books

Hall, Barbara and Mather, Jenni: *Australian Women Photographers 1840–1960*. Greenhouse Publications, 1986.

Walling, Edna: *Gardens in Australia*. Oxford University Press, second edition, 1944.

Walling, Edna: *Cottage and Garden in Australia*. Geoffrey Cumberlege, Oxford University Press, first edition, 1947.

Walling, Edna: *A Gardener's Log*. Geoffrey Cumberlege, Oxford University Press, first edition, 1948.

Watts, Peter: *The Gardens of Edna Walling*. The Women's Committee of the National Trust of Australia (Victoria), first edition, 1981.

Other Sources

La Trobe Collection, State Library of Victoria.

Australian Hotel Co. Ltd, Sydney: "The Australian Handbook", winter 1939: "An Adventure in Rural Development", by Edna Walling.

Australian Home Beautiful.

"The Conservation of Sites and Structures of Historical and Archaeological Significance in the Upper Yarra Valley and Dandenong Ranges Region", by Mark Roger Tansley.

Unpublished notes of Edna Walling in the possession of Margaret Hendry.

Unpublished notes of Edna Walling in the possession of Peter Watts.